THE
PUBLIC
and
AMERICAN
FOREIGN
POLICY,
1918-1978

By the same author

AMERICAN OPINION AND THE RUSSIAN ALLIANCE,
1939–1945

CARROLL COUNTY, MARYLAND: A HISTORY,
1837–1976 (co-author)

FOREIGN
POLICY
ASSOCIATION
1918

THIS BOOK IS ABOUT THAT VAST ASSORTMENT OF AMERICANS —plain citizens along with the great and powerful—whose efforts, pressures, hopes, and fears have entered into the mosaic of the nation's foreign policy. As Professor Levering shows, American foreign policy has never been the exclusive preserve of the elite. Innumerable citizens have applied their energies to studying, debating, and influencing its course according to their varied interests and their ideas of what is right.

This project was initiated by the editors of the Foreign Policy Association to mark its sixtieth anniversary year. Since 1918 FPA has been dedicated to helping concerned Americans—students and mature citizens—increase their knowledge of the world of nations and of U.S. foreign policy. Appropriately, then, this book is a study of their opinions and activities, and of their interaction with the policy-makers, over the six historic decades since, as the author says, "the United States indisputably became a world power."

By implication, the book is also a tribute to these citizen auxiliaries of foreign policy-making, whose striving reflects not merely self-interest narrowly conceived, but often also a passionate concern for the nation, for human values, and for free debate. Its sponsors hope it will contribute to a wider knowledge of the foreign policy role of the American citizen, in whose hands the control of the public policies of the United States ultimately rests.

—THE EDITORS

THE
PUBLIC
and
AMERICAN
FOREIGN
POLICY,
1918-1978

by
RALPH B. LEVERING

Published for the Foreign Policy Association by
WILLIAM MORROW AND COMPANY, INC.
NEW YORK   1978

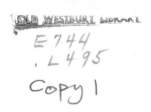
Copyright © 1978 by Foreign Policy Association

Library of Congress Cataloging in Publication Data

Levering, Ralph B
    The public and American foreign policy, 1918-1978.

    Bibliography: p.
    Includes index.
    1. United States—Foreign relations—20th century—Public opinion. 2. Public opinion—United States.
I. Title.
E744.L495   301.15′43′32773   77-28536
ISBN 0-688-03308-3
ISBN 0-688-08308-0 pbk.

BOOK DESIGN   CARL WEISS

Printed in the United States of America.

First Edition

1   2   3   4   5   6   7   8   9   10

FOR SAMUEL

AND MIRIAM LEVERING

FOREWORD

THE FOREIGN POLICY of a democracy cannot be successfully
carried on for very long unless the policy-makers continually
consult public opinion. This simple truth has sometimes been
neglected at great cost. Policy-makers are tempted to brush
aside trends in public opinion which go contrary to what they
plan to do. Or citizens may become discouraged and decide
that their opinions don't count, and that keeping up with
foreign policy developments is a waste of time. Such situations
are dangerous, as we learned in the case of Vietnam.

It is important, therefore, that all concerned should be
aware of the part that public opinion has played in American
foreign policy in our times. That story is the subject of Professor Levering's book.

I believe the role of public opinion in deciding great foreign
policy issues has been constructive and indispensable. This
belief is based on the record of public opinion surveys on
every important policy issue since 1935. This record does not
bear out the idea of so many civil and military leaders who
look on military matters, for instance, as the exclusive prov-
ince of experts, and believe that they can manipulate public
opinion. On the contrary, the record reveals the powerful
impact of *events* on public opinion—especially those events
that grow out of the success or failure of American policies.

Public opinion changes in a logical manner as the public

continuously casts up the balance. Quite often the public is ahead of the leadership. For example, prior to World War II the public saw the threat of Nazi Germany before many of their leaders did. They were also ahead of the leadership in calling for increased air power.

Many years later, in the early stages of our involvement in Vietnam, the public seemed to sense far ahead of our military leaders that it would be difficult to win this kind of war. Within months after the Gulf of Tonkin incident of 1964, many were predicting "another Korea." The public early accepted the idea of turning the fighting over to the Vietnamese in what much later became the official Vietnamization policy. The military experts were reluctant to move in this direction, but public opinion put pressure on the political leaders who, in turn, put pressure on the military.

Public opinion is certainly not infallible, but when the people have enough information about alternative policies and the reasons behind each, they usually have the good sense to pick the best. In any event where people feel that their important interests are at stake, they will insist on their right to participate in policy decisions. It is extremely important that our foreign policy leaders understand this necessity, take pains to inform the people accurately, and give due weight to their views. This may add to the difficulty of policy-making, but in no other way can we achieve wisdom and steadiness in the foreign policy of our country, which seems destined to remain for a long time to come at the hinge of world history.

—GEORGE GALLUP

PREFACE

THE AMERICAN PEOPLE have long been condemned not only for the sins of conformity and materialism but also for their alleged adverse effect on the conduct of the nation's foreign policy. Such distinguished students of international relations as George F. Kennan, Walter Lippmann, and Hans Morgenthau have denounced public involvement in American foreign policy. The public was blamed in the 1920s for being too chauvinistic, in the 1930s for being too isolationist, in the 1950s for being too moralistic, and in the 1960s for being too militaristic. It has been blamed for America's failure to join the League of Nations and the World Court, for its failure to permit the government to take steps to halt Japanese, Italian, and German aggression in the 1930s, and for permitting the United States to continue its large-scale involvement in the Indochina War for nearly a decade.

While recognizing the importance of public opinion in American foreign policy, critics of public involvement have tended to overlook the strong influence that governmental officials can have on public opinion. During World War II, for example, the Roosevelt administration helped to develop generally favorable attitudes toward Russia; after the war, the Truman administration helped to create and solidify the image of Russia as an enemy of the United States. In seeking to influence public opinion, officials often have received invaluable assistance from the news media, which normally devote much of their coverage of foreign affairs to transmitting information about official policies and the rationales for them. Presidents and other officials have been affected by public opinion, especially when opinions have been strongly held and when organizations have articulated them forcefully. But American officials also have been able to build public support for new initiatives in foreign policy.

In this study I attempt to provide an overview of public involvement in foreign policy issues in the years since 1918, when as part of the victorious coalition in World War I the United States indisputably became a world power. I concentrate on describing broad perspectives toward foreign policy and on analyzing attitudes toward particular nations and foreign policy issues among both the general public and the small percentage of Americans who are foreign policy activists at any given time. For the attitudes of the general public, I have relied primarily on public opinion polls; for the attitudes of foreign policy activists, I have studied the writings of involved individuals and especially the work of organizations which have sought to influence American policy. Because this book is a broad survey, it is based largely on secondary sources and published public opinion data.

In the first chapter, which is based on my own research and that of many other historians and social scientists, I discuss the nature of the public and the major reasons for differences and similarities in the public's approach to foreign policy issues. In the next four chapters, which are basically chronological, I treat the changing distribution of opinion on foreign policy issues since 1918 both within the general public and among foreign policy activists. In the concluding chapter I assess the impact of the public on foreign policy and the strengths and weaknesses of public involvement in the policy-making process.

Because of the increasing global interdependence which has been the hallmark of the twentieth century, public attitudes toward other nations, assumptions about the objectives of American foreign policy, and efforts to influence specific policies form a central theme of modern American history. Having been asked to write a relatively short book, I obviously have not been able to present an exhaustive treatment of this subject. I hope that many readers will have the interest to examine at least some of the works listed in the selected bibliography and footnotes, and that this book will assist Americans interested in foreign affairs in becoming more aware of the interplay between the public and policy-makers in the making of American foreign policy.

I wish to thank the Foreign Policy Association for its assistance and encouragement. I also appreciate the contributions of those who have read drafts of the manuscript: Richard D. Challener, Wayne S. Cole, John Lewis Gaddis, Patricia Webb Levering, and Arthur S. Link.

The book is dedicated to my parents, Samuel and Miriam Levering, who have worked for more than forty years in organizations seeking to influence American foreign policy and to create foundations for a more just and peaceful world order.

CONTENTS

THE
PUBLIC
and
AMERICAN
FOREIGN
POLICY,
1918-1978

1

THE MANY PUBLICS— AND THE FEW

It must be remembered that "public opinion," "the will of the nation," and phrases of that kind are really nothing but metaphors, for thought and will are attributes of a single mind, and "the public" or "the nation" are aggregates of many minds.

—GEORGE CARSLAKE THOMPSON (1886) [1]

IT IS THE LATE 1940s, at the height of public concern about Russia's international behavior, and the following are five hypothetical American citizens with different degrees of interest, information, and involvement in foreign policy issues:

Citizen A is an editorialist for a major newspaper who writes primarily about international affairs. He has a master's degree in International Relations from Columbia University, he has time to read widely in periodicals like *Foreign Affairs* and current books on international issues, and he participates in Boston's World Affairs Council. He is angered—but not particularly surprised—by Russia's coup in Czechoslovakia, and he does not believe that Stalin intends to attack Western Europe or the United States.

Citizen B also is a college graduate, and she too works hard to keep up on international developments. She participated in local organizations during World War II to build support for American participation in the United Nations, and now she is distressed that the United Nations is proving inadequate to deal with such momentous questions as the control of atomic energy. She is an active member of a rapidly growing organization called United World Federalists, whose ultimate aim is the establishment of an effective world government.

Citizen C completed two years of college before being called to service in World War II. He became interested in foreign policy issues during the debate over American involvement in the late 1930s and early 1940s, and he has continued to try to keep informed. But his work since 1945 as a junior executive in a large department store has occupied most of his time and energy, and he belongs to no organization primarily concerned with foreign policy. But he does read the international news in a metropolitan daily with relatively extensive coverage of foreign affairs, and he also reads *Time* magazine. He believes that Russia threatens the peace he fought for, and that President Truman should be even firmer than he has been.

Citizen D finished high school, got married, and now has two children. During the war she worked as a clerk in an army recruiting center, a temporary position that was eliminated at the end of the war. A Polish-American, she remained highly suspicious of Russia even during the wartime alliance, and now both she and her steelworker husband are angry because Poland has fallen to Communism. She makes no effort to keep up with general foreign policy issues, but she is sensitive to statements and policies relating to Poland.

Citizen E, a hired hand on the same farm for more than thirty years, has a fourth-grade education. He has never read a newspaper regularly, and he has never had any interest in state and national affairs, much less foreign policy issues. The people with whom he associates also have no interest in learning about or discussing foreign affairs.

Citizens A, B, and C belong to what public opinion analysts call the "attentive public," the perhaps 10 to 20 percent of

Americans who are relatively well informed about foreign
policy issues. Citizens D and E belong to the "mass public,"
the great majority of adults who usually pay little or no attention to foreign affairs.

Closer scrutiny, however, reveals the wide range of potential influence on foreign policy even within these categories.
Although Citizens A, B, and C all belong to the "attentive
public," Citizen A also belongs to the minuscule proportion
of the public who can use their direct access to the media to
propagate their foreign policy views. Citizen B is one of the
approximately 5 percent of Americans who belong to non-
partisan organizations whose primary purpose is to influence
public policy. Citizen C, although fairly well informed about
foreign policy issues, probably holds less politically relevant
opinions than Citizen D. Finally, there are obvious problems
in lumping together in the "mass public" both Citizens D and
E; for, unlike Citizen D, Citizen E has no views on foreign
policy issues which politicians and other officials need to
consider.

This brief discussion, in addition to warning against over-
generalization in public-opinion analysis, illustrates a point
made repeatedly by social psychologists: that opinions on
foreign affairs, as on other subjects, are rooted deeply in an
individual's personality and values. Sociologists and political
scientists stress the complementary point that opinions frequently are influenced by social pressures and the dominant
perspectives of organizations to which a person belongs.
Viewed historically, the four most important influences on
public perceptions of American foreign policy in the twentieth century, specific events aside, have been quantity and
quality of education, patterns of media usage, ethnic affiliation, and party affiliation. Three other factors often considered
by public opinion analysts—religion, regionalism, and economic differences—are less helpful in explaining differing
perspectives on American foreign policy.[2]

Because most foreign policy issues are quite complex and

require at least some background knowledge about the countries involved, it is not surprising that college graduates—especially those with broad, liberal arts training—consistently have possessed the most interest in, information about, and willingness to act on foreign policy issues. Only 3 percent of college graduates in a poll in the late 1940s were unaware of the Marshall Plan, for example, whereas 29 percent of those with grammar school training or less were unaware of it. If one could know only one thing about a respondent to a public opinion question on foreign policy, the most useful information would be the amount of his formal education.[3]

Although education clearly is correlated with information about foreign affairs, high educational achievement does not imply dissent from official policy. On the contrary, support for such post-World War II policies as the Marshall Plan and NATO was greatest among the highly educated, and college graduates were also the strongest supporters of the increasingly unpopular wars in Korea and Vietnam. According to John E. Mueller, the better educated tend to possess "a comparatively close identification with the nation, its leadership, and its destiny; an awareness of and a sympathy for the problems of dealing with other countries in a unified manner; and, consequently, a susceptibility to leadership appeals on issues of international policy." [4]

Finally, the better educated tend to adapt their opinions to changes in the international situation faster and more completely than does the average person. During World War II, for example, the better educated developed more favorable attitudes toward Russia during 1942 and 1943 than did the less educated; but the better educated also recognized the rifts in the Grand Alliance and turned against Russia more quickly in 1945 and 1946. By 1970, when American policy toward mainland China clearly was becoming more conciliatory, 52 percent of the college educated believed that the Peking regime should be admitted to membership in the United Nations. Only 32 percent of the high school group and 26 percent of the grade school group favored admission.[5]

Because most Americans receive virtually all of their information about foreign affairs directly from the news media or indirectly from friends who follow the news more closely than they do, differences in the use of news media are highly significant in understanding opinions on foreign policy issues. Newspapers differ substantially in the quality of foreign policy coverage, as anyone who has read both *The New York Times* and the New York *Daily News* on the same day can attest. But newspapers can treat foreign policy stories in much greater detail than can radio and television, and periodicals can provide even more thorough news analysis on particular issues.

In the early twentieth century the "mass public" received almost all of its news from newspapers, and the "attentive public" supplemented newspapers with magazines like the *New Republic, Atlantic Monthly,* and *Literary Digest.* Sociologists Robert S. and Helen Merrell Lynd found that newspapers were still the most important medium in "Middletown" in the mid-1930s, but radio had developed rapidly since the mid-1920s. Since World War II the "mass public" has received most of its news from the electronic media, supplemented by newspapers, whereas the "attentive public" has emphasized magazines and newspapers. In the mid-1940s, 62 percent of grammar-school-educated men received most of their news from radio, compared with only 39 percent of college-educated men. A study in the late 1960s found that 40 percent of college graduates and 50 percent of those with "some college" were most dependent for news on periodicals, whereas those with high school degrees or less depended on television and radio. Only 2 percent of the high school graduates depended on periodicals. Newspapers were second in importance for all groups.[6]

Patterns of media usage are influenced above all not by the amount of education, but by the value of particular kinds of information to the individual. If people believe that they can influence events outside their communities, if their orientation is toward the broader world rather than being limited to events in their communities, and if they have a circle of friends and belong to organizations in which foreign policy issues are discussed, they are much more likely to make the effort to keep informed about foreign affairs than are those who lack the personal and social incentives for doing so. Perhaps that is why continuing interest in foreign affairs has been found most frequently in large urban areas and university communities.[7]

The third important correlate of attitudes toward foreign policy issues has been party affiliation, which for most people has been acquired from parents as an important aspect of political socialization. In the bipartisan atmosphere of the mid- to late 1940s, there was relatively little difference in the foreign policy preferences of those who identified themselves as Democrats or Republicans. But at other times, such as in attitudes toward President Roosevelt's interventionist policies before Pearl Harbor or in attitudes toward President Truman's conduct of foreign policy during the Korean War, there have been sharp partisan differences. When asked in 1951 whether they were "generally satisfied or dissatisfied with the way the United States has been acting toward other countries," 48 percent of Democrats as opposed to only 24 percent of Republicans were satisfied. When asked the more specific question of whether they supported President Truman or General MacArthur in their dispute over how to conduct the Korean War, 47 percent of Democrats supported Truman and 42 percent supported MacArthur, whereas only 7 percent of Republicans supported Truman while a whopping 82 percent supported MacArthur. During the Vietnam War, Democrats were more inclined than Republicans to support the war during the Johnson years, but the situation was reversed during the Nixon years.[8]

Just as the better informed "attentive public" do not tend to be more critical of official policy than the "mass public," so the better informed can be at least as partisan in their outlook as the average citizen. During the Korean War, for example, well-informed Democrats gave strong support to Truman administration policies in general and Truman's position regarding MacArthur in particular, whereas well-informed Republicans were the most sharply critical of Truman's foreign policy and his position in the dispute with MacArthur. Those Republicans and Democrats with "low" and "medium" levels of information divided less sharply; in fact, they often were closer to each other in viewpoint than they were to the very partisan views of those Republicans and Democrats with "high" levels of information. An explanation for these differences is that the better informed are much more aware of partisan differences during periods of interparty conflict, and they tend to identify with leaders like Secretary of State Dean Acheson and Senator Robert Taft who articulate these differences.[9]

Because modern public opinion polling did not begin until the mid- to late 1930s, relatively little is known about the foreign policy attitudes of the Republican and Democratic rank-and-file during the interwar period. But the biggest single reason for the defeat of American membership in the League of Nations was that Republican Senator Henry Cabot Lodge had more votes in the Senate for his position than did Democratic President Woodrow Wilson, and Republican Senators were most influential in defeating proposals for American involvement in the World Court and in passing and seeking to defend the neutrality legislation of the mid-1930s. Because leading isolationist Senators of both parties generally were not defeated for re-election until after the Japanese attack on Pearl Harbor discredited isolationism, it seems safe to conclude that opposition to internationalist measures was not a political liability during the interwar years.

Last but definitely not least among the central correlates of attitudes toward foreign policy has been ethnic affiliation. As late as 1950 there were nearly 11 million foreign-born persons in the United States plus nearly 24 million others with at least one foreign-born parent. In 1918, in the wake of the massive immigration in the two decades prior to the outbreak of World War I, the percentage of recent immigrants and those with foreign-born parents was considerably higher. Although the percentage of immigrants and children of immigrants has declined steadily during the past sixty years, ethnic consciousness has remained strong in many groups.[10]

Many immigrants have maintained significant ties with the old country. Because of these ties, and because some of their former compatriots have wanted to use immigrants to raise funds and to influence American foreign policy toward their countries, immigrants frequently have championed policies favorable to their former homelands. Among the groups with the greatest impact on aspects of American foreign policy since 1918 have been Irish-Americans and German-Americans among the "older" ethnic groups, and Jewish-Americans, Italian-Americans, Polish-Americans, and Greek-Americans among the ethnic groups whose great migration to America came at the turn of the twentieth century.

Particular ethnic groups have been most effective when they have achieved a large measure of internal unity, when they have developed lobbying organizations to present their viewpoint to public officials and the press, and when there have been few countervailing pressures on policy-makers. Americans of East European descent, for example, assisted in the development and perpetuation of a strong anti-Russian policy in the 1940s and 1950s at a time when there were few domestic pressures for a more conciliatory policy. American Jews, well-organized and aided by general public indifference to the issue, were instrumental in establishing Israel and getting the Truman administration to support it. In contrast, the efforts of many German-Americans to maintain American neutrality in the two world wars failed in the face of strong countervailing pressures, not the least of which were the pro-British proclivities of many Americans of English and Scotch-Irish descent.

Although analysis of poll results on the basis of religion sometimes has been useful on such domestic issues as attitudes toward legalizing abortions, it generally has been of little value on foreign policy issues. For many Catholics, ethnic background probably has been a more important determinant of foreign policy opinions than their Catholicism. For Protestants, the term "Protestant" is itself a thoroughly unsatisfactory designation; much more useful would be "Episcopalian," "Seventh Day Adventist," or "Southern Baptist." In any case, although religious beliefs and organizational affiliation probably have been important in determining the foreign policy outlook of a small minority of Americans, there is no evidence to suggest that religion has been as persistent a determinant of foreign policy opinions as the four major correlates discussed previously.[11]

A few exceptions to this generalization should be mentioned. Religion has played a crucial role for such generally pacifist sects as Quakers, Brethren, and Mennonites. Foreign policy issues became focal points of differences of opinion in the 1950s and 1960s within such Protestant organizations as the National Council of Churches, and between this organization and other Protestant groups. The Black Muslims and some other black religious sects have preached solidarity with some African and Arab states. And the Catholic Church apparently had strong influence upon its members in regard to support for General Francisco Franco during and after the Spanish civil war. But on broad issues of foreign policy, the Catholic leadership generally has not sought to impose specific foreign policy positions on the average Catholic.

Nor has regionalism been a major source of foreign policy views for most Americans. Close examination of votes in Congress apparently dividing along regional lines often reveals that they can be explained more convincingly as partisan or ideological splits, and regional differences in public opinion results almost always can be explained more convincingly by one or a combination of the four major influences discussed above.

The most famous example of regional differences—the South's "internationalism" and the Midwest's "isolationism" before World War II—is best explained not by broad generalizations about alleged regional character traits, but by reference to partisan and ethnic differences. In the 1930s the South was solidly Democratic, and it supported President Roosevelt on foreign policy just as it had supported President Wilson a generation before. Except for blacks, who were still largely disfranchised, Southerners were overwhelmingly English or Scotch-Irish in ethnic background, and hence tended to identify with Great Britain. The Midwest, by contrast, was traditionally Republican and contained large numbers of Americans of German and Swedish background who opposed "fighting for England." [12]

Finally, economic differences generally have not been important determinants of attitudes toward most foreign policy issues. Levels of income have tended to correspond to levels of educational achievement. Where there have been differences in foreign policy views among upper-, middle-, and lower-class respondents, analysis of poll data suggests that these almost always have had more to do with differences in education, use of media, and political affiliation than with differences in income. Although occupational differences have affected attitudes toward tariffs and other issues of international economics, levels of information and political and ethnic affiliations have been far more important sources of most foreign policy views.[13]

Balancing the centrifugal forces whose effects on public attitudes toward foreign policy I have been discussing up to now, however, are strong centripetal ones. Despite the strong differences of opinion over entry into the League of Nations, over involvement in World War II, over the "loss" of Eastern Europe and China, and over Vietnam, as well as over domestic issues, the nation coheres. Its coherence results from values which the great majority of Americans hold in common, values reflected in the practices of the government, the press, and interest groups. If from some perspectives there are "many" publics whose diverse interests and actions could not permit a coherent foreign policy, from other perspectives there are "few" publics which aid in the definition of the major foreign policy issues facing the nation at any given time.

One centripetal factor permitting the administration in power leeway in developing its approach to foreign policy is general public indifference to most foreign policy issues. The "attentive public" generally is composed of no more than 15 percent of the adult population, and even within this group only a small percentage is involved at any given time in lobbying, letter writing, or other activities intended to influence foreign policy. Unless an ethnic or economic interest is threatened, or war seems imminent or peace seems overdue, the other 85 percent tend to leave foreign policy to the President, Congress, and the bureaucracy—at least until the next election.

The government also benefits from a strong, deeply ingrained patriotism, a patriotism based on pride in institutions as well as love of homeland. Most Americans are proud of their system of government, and they accept its stalemates and frustrations. To them the United States is the best place in the world to live. The darker side of this feeling—that foreigners are inferior and worthy of contempt—has not been limited to the Hearst and McCormick newspapers of the 1920s and 1930s. This deep-seated patriotism is a major reason why most Americans have given strong support to their government not only when the country was attacked in 1941 but also in 1917, 1950, and 1965 when it became involved in major wars without being directly attacked. And although skepticism increased as a result of repeated deceptions during

Vietnam and Watergate, the general public rallied around President Ford during the *Mayaguez* affair in 1975 as it had for President Kennedy during the Cuban missile crisis in 1962. Centrifugal tendencies are checked not only by this large and common fund of patriotism but also by the fact that all groups in society, including the government, work within a climate of opinion based on the dominant assumptions of a particular historical period. I shall argue in subsequent chapters that the dominant assumptions for the interwar period were established by 1920, that those for the 1940s were established by 1941, that those for the 1950s and 1960s were established by 1952, and that those for the 1970s were established by 1972. Although one might quibble over the exact years in which the dominant assumptions changed, it is clear that these assumptions have circumscribed the range of policy options given serious consideration by officials and the public.

The babble of voices and multiplicity of perspectives emanating from a large and diverse nation also are checked in practice by the establishment of priorities within an administration and the definition of news by the mass media. An administration tends to focus on a few issues—reciprocal trade and neutrality during Franklin Roosevelt's first administration, for example, or relations with the Soviet Union, the Middle East, and southern Africa during Jimmy Carter's first year. Issues outside these priority areas tend to be ignored. Similarly, the press tends to devote no more than 10 percent of its space to foreign policy issues, and hence must be highly selective in its emphasis. Generally, the foreign policy issues which administration officials emphasize and which members of Congress debate become the foci of media coverage of foreign policy as well.[14]

The result is that organizations specializing in foreign affairs are much more effective in influencing public opinion and governmental policy at some times than at others. The books and pamphlets issued by the Council on Foreign Relations, the Foreign Policy Association, and the League of

Nations Association advocating measures for collective security almost certainly had a greater impact in 1940 than in 1935. Conversely, the success of Dorothy Detzer, the Washington lobbyist for the Women's International League for Peace and Freedom, in convincing Senator Nye in 1934 to conduct the munitions hearings contrasts with the comment to her by an opposing lobbyist after both had listened to President Roosevelt's speech on December 8, 1941, requesting a declaration of war against Japan. "How's peace?" he inquired. The substantial influence of the "China lobby" in the 1950s similarly contrasts with its relative impotence during the Kissinger-Nixon visits to Peking in the early 1970s.[15]

In sum, most Americans, having limited knowledge about foreign affairs, usually have looked to their President and other officials for guidance in foreign affairs. In normal times the government, though never totally immune to appeals from citizens' and pressure groups, has set the basic foreign policy agenda and has used the media to convey that agenda to the public. But when the governmental elites become seriously divided, as during the League of Nations controversy or the Vietnam War, large segments of the public become involved in foreign policy debates. From these periods of serious division have emerged changing assumptions which have affected the conduct of American foreign policy.

Ideally, public opinion in a democracy should be enlightened by governmental leaders and the media; the wishes of this enlightened public should be conveyed clearly to the leaders; and the leaders, as they fashion specific policies, should keep in mind the broad outlines of public sentiment. The reality is that there are major obstructions along the channel of communication from government to the people, and along the one from the people to the government. There also is the reality that, even if the obstructions did not exist, the communications themselves often are based on insufficient knowledge and tainted by partisan motives.

A good place to begin in pointing out weaknesses in the public opinion–foreign policy cycle is with the public. The great majority—the "mass public"—is almost always most interested in personal lives and careers, secondarily in friends and community, third in state and national domestic issues, and last in foreign policy issues. When foreign policy issues infringe on personal concerns, as in the late 1930s and in the late 1960s, interest in foreign policy issues grows dramatically, but even at the height of World War II public opinion analyst Hadley Cantril reported that "the intensity of public interest in domestic affairs is almost twice as great as the intensity of public interest in foreign affairs." Lack of interest has led to lack of information. In 1942, after five years of fighting between Japanese and American-supported Chinese soldiers and at a period of crisis in Britain's colonial rule in India, 60 percent of a sample of adult Americans could not locate either China or India on an outline map.[16]

To develop informed opinions on most foreign policy issues requires more effort than spending an average of about two minutes per day reading stories on foreign policy issues in daily newspapers and listening to news roundups on radio or television; yet that is all the time the average American devotes to learning about foreign affairs. According to Alfred O. Hero, Jr., no more than 1 percent of adult Americans in the late 1950s "read regularly or frequently about world issues in the better analytical, relatively profound, semi-popular periodicals, such as the *New York Times* (Sunday edition), *Christian Science Monitor, Harper's, Atlantic, New Republic, Current History,* the Headline Series [published by the Foreign Policy Association], and *Foreign Affairs* . . ."[17]

In addition to lacking information and an analytical context in which to place it, the public as a whole permits its views on foreign policy to be shaped by highly personal considerations: family background, the strongly held views of a friend or teacher, biases against particular nations picked up subconsciously in popular magazines and novels, the convictions of a commentator or politician with whom one agrees on domestic issues. These scattered pieces of information and opinion must then pass through "opacities and magnifications in the individual's outlook on his world." The psychological tendency is to bend incoming messages to fit preconceived images or, as Walter Lippmann wrote in his classic *Public Opinion*: "For the most part, we do not first see, and then define, we define first and then see." [18]

The public conveys its foreign policy opinions to policy-makers primarily through three highly imperfect instruments: polls, organizations, and votes. Public opinion polls on foreign policy issues usually require a response of "Yes," "No," or "No opinion" to a set question which may be irrelevant to the way in which a respondent approaches an issue. Most poll results also reveal nothing about the intensity with which positive or negative opinions are held. A minority which feels strongly about an issue such as gun control or Communism in China may have more political significance than a majority with a different viewpoint for whom the issue lacks salience. Finally, poll results often provide little or no insight into the actual policy preferences of the public. Polls are most useful when large numbers of questions about a particular issue have been asked or when the same question has been asked over a period of time, thus permitting the analyst to compare re-sponses to different questions and to study trends in opinion.[19]

Organizations also mobilize segments of public opinion on foreign policy, but the claims of leaders of organizations about opinion on particular issues are much less reliable than poll results. Such organizations as the AFL-CIO, the American Legion, and the United States Chamber of Commerce often claim to speak for millions of members on specific foreign policy issues; in fact, the members of mass organizations gen-erally disagree sharply among themselves. Again a basic ques-tion is salience: how important is membership in any par-ticular organization to an individual, and to what extent does the organization influence an individual's opinions? The fact that most people have several organizational affiliations—corporation or union, church, ethnic association, and so on—makes it very difficult for politicians to gauge the importance of any one organization.

Despite the great effort devoted to studying elections, there perhaps never will be conclusive answers to the question of the precise effects of foreign policy issues even in elections in which these issues seemed to be important, such as 1940 and 1952. Most specialists are convinced that domestic issues usually are considerably more important to voters than foreign policy issues, but it is highly unlikely that Roosevelt would have been elected four times without the intercession of World War II, and close elections like those of 1960 and 1968 may well have been decided, in the last analysis, by dissatisfaction over American foreign policy. Presidents and Congressmen usually have difficulty in gauging the foreign policy implications of the vote in the last election, and they never can know for sure how their foreign policy actions will affect their chances in subsequent elections.

Do the poll results, interest-group resolutions, and other clues to public attitudes get through to foreign policy officials? The answer varies with the official involved, but there is strong evidence that most Presidents since the 1930s have paid close attention to polls, whereas Congressmen and State Department officials often have relied primarily on newspaper editorials or lobbyists as guides to public opinion. The perceptual framework is crucial: some officials are predisposed to value polls or letters from constituents, while others discount them; some politicians have overestimated the strength of particular interest groups, while others have ignored them. In general, officials have approached indicators of public attitudes more intuitively than systematically.[20]

The remainder of the cycle—the distribution of information from the government to the public—takes place primarily through the mass media and secondarily through interest groups, government publications, and direct contact between officials and private citizens. Private organizations regularly provide forums for officials both as speakers for meetings and as contributors to publications. Since 1941 the government has produced many thousands of films, radio tapes, and booklets dealing with topics ranging from international organization to fallout shelters, from the China "White Paper" to *Why Vietnam?* Despite the availability of television, Presidents and other officials still choose to make appearances and solicit support in person throughout the country.

The primary source of information about foreign policy issues continues to be the mass media, for which public policy is only one of several major concerns. The electronic media emphasize entertainment, as do a large proportion of magazines, and newspapers fill most of their space with advertising, sports, comics, fashion, and human interest stories.

Although specific newspapers, magazines, and radio and television news programs vary widely in quality, the media's general approach to coverage of major issues, an approach heavily influenced by entertainment values, is an important factor in understanding the ignorance of much of the public on foreign policy issues. Primary among news values are violence and natural disasters, and close behind are disagreements among famous personalities, international crises, and bizarre events. Because of these news values and limited space, most news about foreign countries relates to violence or the threat of violence, and most news about foreign policy issues in Washington involves either charges and countercharges among political leaders or rewritings of speeches by the President (the nation's most prominent personality) and other leaders. In general, as the Commission on Freedom of the Press pointed out in 1947, "the press emphasizes the exceptional rather than the representative, the sensational rather than the significant." [21]

Newspapers and the electronic media have enabled modern Presidents to present their major foreign policy positions to the public, and they also have permitted spokesmen of the opposition party to state their positions. But they have succeeded much more often in highlighting conflicts than in explaining the background and significance of international issues. Only recently have the wire services begun to offer news analyses regularly, and only recently has there been much emphasis on international economic issues and on social conditions within nations abroad. Even today, as during World War I and its aftermath, the public is at least as likely to encounter in the media sensational, unsubstantiated charges as it is to find the views of lifelong specialists on particular international issues.

Although newspapers, magazines, and the electronic media seldom explain the context of events abroad, they do convey some sense of the administration's general priorities in foreign policy and of opposition to particular policies. They also help to focus public attention—to transform the many publics into the few—by providing a guide to what foreign policy issues the public should be thinking about. Provided with information about major trends in foreign policy, the public can choose to remain uninvolved or it can seek to influence the direction of American policy. Despite their weaknesses, the media have been the most important link between officials and the public in the formulation of American foreign policy.

2

THE DOMINANCE OF DOMESTIC CONCERNS, 1918–1936

The feeling of continental security and of aloofness from Europe had been dominant in the United States for so long that when the World War was over the public were predisposed towards accepting the idea that they had blundered into it or been manoeuvred into it, and that they could easily stay out of similar entanglements in the future if only their government would mind its own business and not be enticed into taking part in collective efforts to save the world.

—ALLEN W. DULLES and
HAMILTON FISH ARMSTRONG (1936) [1]

WORLD WAR I profoundly affected American attitudes toward foreign policy for a generation and established the basic framework in which foreign policy issues have been debated ever since. Entering the war in April 1917 confident that American participation would defeat German autocracy and establish a harmonious, democratic world, most Americans had concluded by 1920 that little or nothing had been gained and that foreign nations were as venal and self-centered as ever.

1918: Rejoicing as World War I ended was soon followed by controversy over the nation's role as a world power.

United Press International

Memories of the dashed hopes of 1917 and 1918 and the domestic turmoil and bitter debate over the League of Nations in 1919 and 1920 haunted Americans in the interwar years. "As long as the memory of that war remains," a public opinion analyst wrote in the late 1930s, "the people will insist that their government go to great lengths to avoid any future conflict." [2]

Beyond generating a strong mood of noninterventionism among the mass public, World War I and its aftermath spawned groups among the attentive public with diverse perspectives on foreign policy, perspectives which have continued to compete for public favor. Supporting cooperation with the League of Nations and collective security against potential aggressors were such groups as the Council on Foreign Relations (founded in 1918 as a discussion group in New York and transformed in 1921 into the current organization) and the Foreign Policy Association (founded in 1918 as the League of Free Nations Association). Whereas these two became primarily educational organizations in the 1920s, the League of Nations Association actively sought American membership in the League during the interwar period. A second perspective, strongest among business and governmental elites, has been called "independent internationalism." Because the United States emerged from World War I as the world's premier economic power, it had the responsibility— and the opportunity—to organize a stable international economic order. Efforts to maintain prosperity and to derive maximum benefit from America's unequaled economic power were at least as important objectives for American foreign policy as were efforts to develop institutions designed to provide collective security. A third perspective, strong in many churches in the 1920s and 1930s, was essentially pacifist; it was represented at the national level by such highly active organizations as the National Council for the Prevention of War and the Women's International League for Peace and Freedom. The fourth major perspective, virulently nationalist but generally noninterventionist, was represented in newly formed veterans groups such as the American Legion and the Veterans of Foreign Wars, in old-line patriotic societies such as the Daughters of the American Revolution, and in important newspapers such as Robert R. McCormick's *Chicago Tribune* and William Randolph Hearst's *San Francisco Examiner.* The nationalist, pacifist, and business perspectives dominated public thinking about foreign affairs in the 1920s and 1930s, but American involvement in World War II brought the supporters of collective security to the forefront.

The person most responsible for establishing the concept of collective security as a major perspective was Woodrow Wilson, a towering figure in American and world affairs during and after World War I. It was Wilson who called the country in 1917 to enter the war to defeat German autocracy and "make the world safe for democracy," who challenged the world in 1918 to make a just and lasting peace, and who insisted in 1919 that the United States enthusiastically join the League of Nations. Because of his failure in the League fight, it is easy to forget that Wilson was an inspiring wartime leader and that the League he fought to establish at the peace conference brought the concept of collective security indelibly into American thinking about world affairs.

It is also easy to criticize Wilson's relationship with the public during these years. Wilson, it has been alleged, permitted George Creel's Committee on Public Information to incite hatred of "the Hun" and of domestic dissenters far more than was necessary; his "Fourteen Points" and other pronouncements were too idealistic and raised false hopes among American liberals and among ethnic groups anxious to see their former homelands achieve their demands at the peace conference; he unwisely called for the election of a Democratic Congress in the fall of 1918 and failed to appoint any prominent Republicans as delegates to the peace conference; and he stubbornly refused to accept Senator Henry Cabot

Lodge's reservations as a basis for American entry into the League of Nations even after it became clear that the public could not "force" the Senate to accept Wilson's League. During the war Wilson did underestimate the difficulties of constructing a peace settlement that would reflect the ideals that he and other American liberals of the period cherished and that also would satisfy the conflicting goals of the victors and the vanquished, the colonial powers and the peoples aspiring to nationhood. And Wilson's political instincts, which generally had served him well for more than five years in the White House, did fail him after victory in the war was assured in the fall of 1918. But what is most significant about the World War I period is not Wilson's successes and failures, but the breathtaking rapidity of change, the sense that events were out of control, the feeling that, as Mark Sullivan put it, the "equilibrium" of the pre-war international order had shifted to "a world out of balance." [3]

Between 1917 and 1920 most Americans grew to dislike increasing numbers of foreign countries. After the Bolsheviks overthrew the Provisional Government in Russia in the fall of 1917, virtually the entire American press began denouncing Lenin's government. This campaign against those "enemies of civilization" who were thwarting the democratic impulses of the Russian people occurred not only on the editorial pages but also on the front pages in stories frequently filled with such inaccuracies as the claim that the Bolsheviks were "German agents" or that they were "nationalizing women" for their own pleasure as part of their assault on civilized values. After the Russians accepted the harsh German terms of peace, there were persistent demands for American and Allied military intervention in Russia against the Bolsheviks, ostensibly for the purpose of preventing them from helping Germany. When the American government announced in August 1918 that troops had been sent to Russia the previous month, its official explanation was devious and lacking in credibility. But the action was disapproved only by radicals and by some liberals, and even after Germany was defeated Americans were divided as to whether the nation's troops aiding the "Whites" in the Russian civil war should be removed. The United States continued to withhold diplomatic recognition from "godless" Russia after the last troops finally were withdrawn in March 1920.[4]

Most Americans—even most of the more attentive—were unable to comprehend the meaning of the Communist revolution in Russia. They assumed that Lenin and his associates could not mean what they said, and that changes in the economic system, for example, could not work because they violated immutable economic laws. But Americans were able to understand the emphasis on national self-interest which the Allied powers displayed in the embarrassing "secret treaties" detailing the division of the spoils of war in the event of Allied victory, and in the jockeying for advantage at the peace conference. The British declined to give immediate independence to Ireland, the French demanded too harsh a peace against Germany, and the Italians and the upstart Japanese insisted upon territorial concessions. Most Americans, convinced of their nation's superiority and devotion to principle, grew weary by late 1919 of having allies like these.

The idea that an association of nations should be established after the war to prevent the recurrence of such senseless slaughter was propagated even before American entry by the League to Enforce Peace and other organizations, but it did not become an official American war aim until it became Wilson's fourteenth point in his famous address to Congress on January 8, 1918. At that time it was not controversial: everyone wanted peace to be preserved after the war and the more attentive knew that the leaders of the League to Enforce Peace were solid conservatives like former President William Howard Taft.

From January until the war ended on November 11, 1918, the public generally was more concerned about defeating Germany and combating Bolshevism than about the specifics of Wilson's peace program, including the League. But a small group of prominent liberals began to meet in the spring of 1918 to support Wilson's ideals, and by the time the much expanded group presented itself to the public shortly after the armistice as the League of Free Nations Association, it was well organized to fight for American membership in the League of Nations.

Despite Wilson's unwise partisanship and his somewhat controversial decision to attend the peace conference himself, active support for an association of nations grew sharply during the early months of 1919. Among the attentive public, interest was so high that approximately one hundred thousand persons applied for the four thousand tickets available when Taft and Wilson spoke at the Metropolitan Opera House in New York on March 4, and forty thousand more sought admission to a public meeting in Boston. In early April the *Literary Digest* published the result of a poll of 1,377 editors across the country which showed that more than half, or 718, favored the League, 181 opposed it, and 478 favored it conditionally. The results of a questionnaire printed in sixteen newspapers suggests that the League was broadly supported among the general population: more than three of every four of the approximately 140,000 respondents expressed support for the League. Reports from religious and economic associations confirmed the existence of broad support among their membership. By the spring of 1919 more than three hundred thousand persons had joined the League to Enforce Peace, and many others belonged to the League of Free Nations Association and other organizations which supported the League. Even Senator Lodge acknowledged that the League enjoyed widespread support.[5]

Although public opinion polls were not conducted until the mid-1930s, one can judge that the strongest supporters of the League tended to be Americans of British descent, Protestants who were members of Episcopal, Presbyterian, Methodist, Quaker, and similar non-fundamentalist churches with close ties to England and Scotland. Inspired by social gospel theology and determined that institutions be established to prevent war in the future, such groups of relatively liberal Protestants as the Federal Council of Churches and the Church Peace Union worked energetically to make American membership in the League a reality. Because of the general *de facto* exclusion of Catholics and Jews from top leadership positions in American society in 1919, the leading Protestant churches counted as members most of those whom public opinion analysts call "influentials." It was these local influentials and their church bodies who insisted up to the final Senate vote in March 1920 that a way had to be found for the United States to join the League.[6]

Those who came to oppose American membership in the League generally waited to see what Wilson achieved at the peace conference before stating their opposition publicly. The opposition was a motley group: conservative nationalists who professed to revere Washington's Farewell Address and the Monroe Doctrine, liberals distressed by the imperfections of the Treaty of Versailles, and ethnic groups such as the Irish-Americans, who claimed that American membership in the League would compel the United States to send troops to aid England in keeping Ireland in the British Empire. The ethnic groups had organizations which could mobilize their opposition politically, and the nationalists formed groups such as the League for the Preservation of American Independence to counter pro-League forces.

Because the Republicans held a slim majority in the Senate, and because ratification would require a two-thirds vote, approximately twenty Republican votes were needed to ratify the Treaty of Versailles. In early 1919 public support of the League seemed so strong that Wilson might secure ratification without having to compromise. As the *New York Times* editorialized in late February, "the opponents of the League, at Washington and elsewhere, will contend in vain against an overwhelming public opinion." By summer, when the terms of

GOING TO TALK TO THE BOSS

1919: With Senate support for the League of Nations dwindling,
President Wilson turned—in vain—to the people for support.

Brown in the *Chicago Daily News*

the treaty had become known and when domestic problems
such as race riots, strikes, and inflation had become acute,
the Republican opponents of the League had gained the backing of several ethnic groups, while the intensity of Protestant
and especially liberal support for the League had decreased.
Wilson's speaking trip on behalf of the League in September
did not lessen Senate resistance to ratifying the League on
the President's terms, but most Republicans and virtually all
Democrats continued to favor ratification either on Wilson's
terms or on Lodge's.[7]

By the fall of 1919, the Republicans did not have to fear
retribution at the polls if the League were defeated so long
as Wilson was viewed as being partially to blame. There were
many ironies in the situation. Wilson, who had been forced to
compromise frequently in Paris in order to get a treaty, now
was refusing to compromise with the Republicans in Washington. And Lodge, a believer in the superiority of English
descent, Protestant religion, and the Republican party, was

now accepting the support of traditionally Democratic Irish-American Catholics and other ethnic groups from eastern and southern Europe whom he held in thinly disguised contempt. The denouement is familiar: the Senate defeated the Treaty of Versailles both with and without the Lodge reservations in November 1919, and, after strong pressure to reconsider from Protestant groups and organizations such as the League of Free Nations Association, the Senate again defeated the treaty with and without reservations in March 1920. Neither Lodge and his supporters nor Wilson and his supporters would compromise sufficiently to pass the treaty and hence permit the United States to join the League of Nations.

Despite being stricken by a major stroke the previous September, Wilson in February 1920 vowed to turn the upcoming presidential election into a "solemn referendum" on the League. The Democratic candidate, James M. Cox, supported the League while his Republican opponent, Warren G. Harding, straddled the issue and won in a landslide. After six years of *Lusitanias,* peace feelers, staggering casualty figures, sacrifice and enforced conformity on the home front, and bickering at Paris and in Washington, most Americans by 1920 wanted nothing more than to be able to forget about foreign affairs and return to "normalcy."

Although Harding chose to interpret the results as being a rejection of American membership in the League, the evidence suggests that the League issue was not a major factor in the campaign. The many publics had many grievances against the Democrats and against "the cock-eyed world," and they voted for a general change in the nation's leadership.

Ever since the Great Depression, images of the 1920s have been dominated by stereotypes of speakeasies where Prohibition was defied, of "flapper" girls who practiced a new morality, of general prosperity symbolized by expensive parties and overnight riches gained on the stock market, and of a narrow-mindedness epitomized in the growth of the Ku Klux

Klan. As for foreign policy, the dominant stereotype has been that Americans in the 1920s retreated into an all-pervasive isolationism and xenophobia.

Personal and domestic concerns undoubtedly were more important to most Americans during the 1920s and early 1930s than were foreign policy issues. With the war over and the question of American entry into the League of Nations carefully avoided by politicians, newspapers and magazines cut back on their coverage of foreign affairs and concentrated on life in the United States in the "New Era." But the war and its aftermath had transformed the nation into the world's greatest economic power and a major military power. And the organizations and attitudes which had grown out of the wartime experience brought foreign policy issues before at least the attentive public quite frequently.

The stereotype of xenophobia has some validity, for there was during the interwar years a strong current of belief in American uniqueness and superiority to foreign nations and peoples. Veterans' groups and patriotic societies propagated this viewpoint vigorously, and politicians up to and including Presidents Harding and Coolidge frequently emphasized the special virtues of Americanism. When 1,100 high school students were asked to appraise the statement, "The United States is superior to all other nations in such important respects as government, educational opportunities, family life and morals," the typical response was one of strong approval. The students also expressed strong support for the Monroe Doctrine, for sending the armed forces to protect American property in Mexico, for excluding the Japanese and Chinese, and for staying out of the League of Nations. When the World Court failed to accept the reservations which the Senate had placed on American membership, the *Cincinnati Enquirer* editorialized on February 11, 1927, that "The reds, pinks and yellows may rave and try to change the situation, but they will find . . . that the color combination loved by the citizenship of America is red, white, and blue." [8]

Studies of local communities in the 1920s and early 1930s also found much evidence of nationalistic feeling. Patriotism and "100% Americanism" were articulated forcefully in the real cities of "Middletown" in Indiana and "Cityville" in New York as well as in famous fictional cities like "Zenith" in the upper Midwest. In "Middletown" a local doctor told a civic club that "Patriotism for our country is the noblest sentiment any man can possess," and a prominent minister declared in a sermon that "The United States is the best country on earth and should give her ideals to the rest of the world." Less noble expressions of patriotism came from spokesmen for such groups as the Ku Klux Klan, who frequently were anti-Catholic and anti-Semitic as well as anti-foreign. The smear word "radicalism" was used against foreign nations like Russia and domestic organizations like labor unions and peace groups.[9]

In the large cities the most effective exponents of intense nationalism were stridently anti-foreign newspapers like the *New York Journal American,* the *Chicago Tribune,* and the *San Francisco Examiner,* and in the 1930s, anti-foreign radio commentators like Father Charles Coughlin and Boake Carter. Taken together, the *de facto* alliance of small-town and urban nationalists and their powerful allies in Congress was able to defeat the campaign of internationalists and peace groups for adherence to the World Court in the mid-1920s and again in the mid-1930s. They also helped to ensure that the United States continued to refuse to recognize Russia until 1933.

The most significant victory for the nationalistic perspective was the successful campaign for immigration restriction, most notably the ending of all Japanese immigration in 1924. The combination of large numbers of first-generation immigrants already living in the United States and the fear that millions more might flock to America in the dislocation following World War I made conditions for comprehensive immigration restriction highly favorable in the early 1920s. The intense nationalism and contempt for southern and eastern

Europeans and especially for Orientals gave both the temporary legislation of 1921 and the permanent immigration law of 1924 a discriminatory bias. Because quotas were based on the proportion of Americans from each foreign nation as of 1890, before the onset of large-scale immigration from southern and eastern Europe, northern and western European nations like Great Britain and Germany were given disproportionately larger quotas than southern and eastern European nations like Italy and Hungary.

Despite pleas from the Coolidge administration to permit Japan to have a quota on the same basis as other nations, a clause for absolute exclusion of Japanese immigrants was included in the 1924 legislation. Exclusion was favored by veterans groups, patriotic societies, some labor organizations, and Congressmen mainly from the South and West. The opposition, which tried to seek a reversal as late as the mid-1930s, included church and internationalist organizations and groups of college students. The exclusion, which received banner headlines in the Japanese press, provided tangible evidence of feelings of American superiority and harmed relations between the two nations.[10]

Whereas the nationalists benefited during the 1920s from strong feelings of patriotism coupled with dislike of foreigners, the pacifists built on the determination of large segments of the public to combat militarism and keep out of foreign wars. Disillusionment with the results of World War I was especially strong among religious leaders who had supported the war effort. "I do not propose to bless war again, or support it, or expect from it any valuable thing," Henry Emerson Fosdick declared. And Rabbi Stephen S. Wise asked his congregation for forgiveness for supporting World War I and promised that "without reservation or equivocation" he would never again support "any war whatsoever." Of 19,372 clergymen who responded to a questionnaire distributed in 1931, 54 percent stated that it was their "present purpose not to sanction any future war or participate as an armed combatant."[11]

In a letter to fellow historian Merle Curti in 1927, Carl L. Becker suggested that the peace movement had become respectable during the campaign for American participation in the League of Nations. At that time it had ceased to be identified solely with religious leaders; it had become acceptable for "business men and lawyers and legislators" to become associated with it. "That is why," Becker concluded, "it is now possible to be a supporter of the League without being dubbed a 'visionary.' " [12]

The peace movement demonstrated such vigor and ingenuity during these years that it could not be totally ignored even by committed nationalists. Having a strong base in the more liberal churches, the peace groups benefited from the dedication and lobbying skills of such leaders as Frederick Libby of the National Council for the Prevention of War, Dorothy Detzer of the Women's International League for Peace and Freedom, and E. Raymond Wilson of the American Friends Legislative Service.

There also was substantial commitment at the grass-roots level to combating militarism and keeping the nation out of future wars. Despite failure in the campaign for American entry into the League of Nations—or perhaps partially because of it—church groups and other organizations, notably women's groups, worked diligently for disarmament measures in the early 1920s. In one of the most energetic citizen action campaigns in American history, dozens of organizations were mobilized in 1921 to support a disarmament conference, and nearly fourteen million letters and petitions were sent to officials, more than ten million of which pleaded for divine intercession in the conference.

A National Council on the Limitation of Armaments was established by leaders of pacifist organizations and such groups as the Foreign Policy Association and the National League of Women Voters to coordinate the campaign. A press service, speaker's bureau, essay contest, and other activities assured that pro-disarmament forces would be heard. When the naval

1933: Activists of the Women's International League for Peace and Freedom rallied in New York for a new cause: disarmament.

United Press International

disarmament treaty went to the Senate for ratification in early 1922, more than sixteen thousand Protestant, Catholic, and Jewish clergy sent a petition to the Senate urging immediate ratification. Although the naval arms limitation agreement probably would have been ratified without such a display of organized support, the peace movement had established itself as an important force in American public life.[13]

The peace lobby continued to be highly visible throughout the 1920s and 1930s. It worked hard for ratification of such measures as the Kellogg-Briand Pact to outlaw war, it lobbied the administration in regard to negotiating positions at disarmament conferences, and it engaged in so many different kinds of activities to maintain public interest in peace and disarmament issues that it would be impossible to list them all. In 1931, for example, the Women's International League for Peace and Freedom, wishing to build support for the Geneva disarmament conference, sponsored a cross-country caravan which visited 130 communities in twenty-five states. Thousands of speeches were made, four hundred thousand signatures for petitions for disarmament were collected, and, as Dorothy Detzer noted later, "the newspapers loved it." [14]

The supporters of at least some form of cooperation with the League, those whom I call "collective security internationalists," were often associated with the peace movement in the public mind and in specific lobbying efforts. But the crucial distinction is that the internationalists in groups like the League of Nations Association, the Foreign Policy Association, and the Council on Foreign Relations generally were not pacifists. They held to the Wilsonian hope that the probability of war could be reduced by international cooperation and by measures for collective security, but they did not renounce the use of force under all conditions.

The leaders of these and such other internationalist organizations as the Carnegie Endowment for International Peace and the World Peace Foundation tended to be concentrated in the Northeast. Twenty-six of the twenty-seven directors of the League of Nations Association in 1929, for example, lived within 300 miles of New York City. And while that organization had three branch offices in the six New England states, it had only an office in Chicago in the eleven-state Middle West. The members of these organizations—men like John Foster Dulles and Thomas W. Lamont—also tended to be Protestants, professionals, and pro-British in outlook.[15]

Although the collective security internationalists and their allies seldom won important legislative fights, such as the effort to have the United States submit disputes to the World Court, they did contribute substantially to the climate of opinion in which the government took steps toward cooperation with international agencies associated with the League. They also flooded libraries, newspaper offices, churches, and governmental agencies with League of Nations documents, semi-scholarly studies of current foreign policy issues and developments elsewhere in the world, and journals like *International Conciliation* and *Foreign Affairs*, which had more than five thousand subscribers within six months after the appearance of the first issue in September 1922. The Foreign Policy Association sponsored frequent luncheon meetings in cities from New York west to Minneapolis and south to Richmond, and provided speakers on foreign policy issues for other groups. These internationalist organizations helped inform an important portion of the attentive public between the wars.[16]

Some of the members of organizations like the Council on Foreign Relations were financiers whose banks in the 1920s organized large loans to governments and private interests abroad. Frequently working with Secretary of Commerce Herbert Hoover and other officials on foreign economic policy, these financiers usually followed the practical approach of independent internationalism, the belief that, in Joan Hoff Wilson's words, "the United States should cooperate on an international scale when it cannot, or does not want to, solve a particular diplomatic problem through unilateral action." Because businessmen and bankers enjoyed great prestige prior to the depression, and because the perceived improbability of a new world war in the 1920s limited the actual impact on policy of the nationalists and pacifists, the business perspective probably had the greatest effect on the day-to-day formulation of American foreign policy.[17]

As with adherents to the other three broad perspectives, one must be careful not to assume that all businessmen supported exactly the same specific policies. International bankers, for example, were much less likely than were small manufacturers in industries facing foreign competition to support the high tariffs contained in the Fordney-McCumber Act of 1922 or the Hawley-Smoot Act of 1930. But most businessmen were less concerned about abstractions like patriotism, pacifism, and collective security than they were about maximizing profits and stabilizing international economic conditions.

If businessmen had been wedded to the ideology of individualism and competitive capitalism that they frequently espoused in articles and after-dinner speeches, one might think that they would have joined the American Legion, the American Federation of Labor, and many Catholic leaders in insisting that the United States continue to shun and denounce Soviet Russia. Instead, conservative businessmen like Henry Ford entered into multimillion dollar contracts with the Communist government, a government which the United States officially did not recognize. Although Ford and some other businessmen believed that American trade and investment might eventually transform Russia's economy into a capitalistic system, their primary motivation clearly was the pragmatic desire to make money. When the Great Depression made the issue of expanding American trade with Russia more urgent, many businessmen joined liberals in pressuring for official recognition. When the Roosevelt administration finally recognized the Soviet Union in November 1933, there was only scattered opposition in nationalistic organs like the *Saturday Evening Post* and the *Chicago Tribune*. The headline in the *Dallas News* epitomized the perspective of many businessmen: "RECOGNITION AID TO SALE OF TEXAS COTTON IN RUSSIA." [18]

One reason why support for establishing diplomatic relations with Russia grew in the early 1930s was the idea that a Russia strengthened by American recognition might serve as a check on Japanese ambitions in the Far East. The peace and prosperity of the late 1920s, symbolized by the Kellogg-Briand Pact of 1928 and a bullish stock market that lasted until the summer of 1929, had given way by 1933 to the reality of Japanese expansionism in Manchuria and China, Adolf Hitler's rise to power in Germany, and the virtual collapse of the American economy. In a book on American foreign policy published in 1930, journalist H. V. Kaltenborn had difficulty in locating any "danger spots" which threatened world peace. Five years later, any person moderately interested in world affairs could have listed several.[19]

Despite the gathering storm clouds on the international horizon, the primary concerns of the American public at least through 1936 were domestic. When would the devastating depression be over? Was Roosevelt concentrating too much power in Washington? Would the Supreme Court affirm the constitutionality of his program? Would there ever be a truce in the war between business and organized labor? In November 1935 only 11 percent of Gallup's respondents named a foreign policy issue as the most important problem facing the nation. Not surprisingly, unemployment and the economy were the major concerns, but "maintaining neutrality" was viewed as the third most important problem.[20]

In the grip of the most serious domestic crisis since the Civil War and even more disillusioned than during the 1920s about the results of World War I, the overwhelming majority of the American people in the early to mid-1930s strongly desired to keep the nation at peace. This desire strengthened the position of the nationalists and the pacifists, both of whom believed that the United States should keep out of foreign quarrels, and further weakened the collective security internationalists. The sarcastic comment of Senator Henrik Shipstead of Minnesota in 1930 was typical of many that were leveled against the advocates of collective security: "To agree to consult is to agree to decide. To agree to decide is to agree to act. To agree to act is to agree that we are going into the next war. They call this the road to peace. That is what they called the Triple Alliance, and the Triple Entente, and the Quadruple Alliance." During the debate on adherence to the World Court in 1935 nationalistic Senator Robert R. Reynolds of North Carolina said that his visits with constituents had convinced him that they had no interest in maintaining peace in "countries of which the great majority had never heard. What do my constituents care about spending money and time and energy and life and blood for the interest of Estonia, Ethiopia, Iraq, Latvia, Liberia?" [21]

The dominant mood in the early 1930s was one of pessimism—pessimism about the prospects for the domestic economy and about the prospects for peace. The League of Nations demonstrated its impotence during the Japanese takeover of Manchuria in 1931 and the subsequent invasion of China, Adolf Hitler vowed to nullify the Treaty of Versailles and Benito Mussolini publicly glorified war, and Britain and France appeared weak and internally divided in comparison with the "dictator" nations. The new Roosevelt administration devoted most of its energies to combating the depression. Its primary goal in foreign policy was the expansion of world trade, the panacea of Secretary of State Cordell Hull. The administration opposed having its freedom of action in foreign affairs limited by neutrality legislation, but it had to yield to some extent in the mid-1930s when Congress, responding to popular pressure and events abroad, passed laws designed to ensure that the nation would not drift into another European war. The neutrality acts of 1935, 1936, and 1937 sought to ensure that no munitions trade with belligerents or travel on belligerent ships would draw the nation into war in the 1930s as they allegedly had in the 1910s.

The prompt passage of the first neutrality act in August 1935 is explained not only by potentially threatening events abroad, such as the prospect of war between Italy and Ethiopia, but also by the work over the previous two years of revisionist historians and peace societies. Articles in popular magazines and books like Walter Millis's *Road to War: America, 1914–1917* argued that American involvement in World War I had been a mistake. Some writers insisted that bankers and munitions manufacturers, profiting from loans and sales to England and France, had led the nation to war, and that the continued involvement of these same groups in international arms traffic increased the danger of American involvement in war in the 1930s. Leaders of the peace movement such as Dorothy Detzer and Frederick Libby, who had hoped until 1932 that disarmament could be achieved by international agreement, now believed that the United States must pass neutrality legislation and take other unilateral steps to keep the nation out of war.[22]

The Senate committee investigating the munitions industries, headed by Senator Gerald P. Nye of North Dakota, also helped to create the atmosphere in which the neutrality laws were passed. This inquiry, spurred by the publication of sensational books and articles in 1934 on the alleged power of munitions makers and by Detzer's personal plea to Nye to head the investigation, created the impression that arms manufacturers exercised vast and sinister power over American foreign policy and that the war-making powers of the executive branch needed to be circumscribed. Nye's conduct of the investigation generally was responsible and restrained, but headline-hungry journalists often resorted to sensationalism in presenting the committee's findings, thus distorting the true significance of its work.[23]

Collective-security internationalists were dismayed by what they viewed as a peace-at-any-price attitude reflected in the neutrality legislation and in general public attitudes toward foreign policy. "The very discussion of neutrality in itself suggests a surrender of the principle that a nation going to war violates the supreme law of a new world community," Clark Eichelberger of the League of Nations Association declared in April 1935. "Can we really presume to determine in 1936 what will be the wise policy to follow in *any and every* international situation which may confront the United States in, say, 1940?" Allen W. Dulles and Hamilton Fish Armstrong of the Council on Foreign Relations asked in a book published in 1936. In their view, the United States had "a continuing responsibility which is broader than the aim to escape from some particular difficulty or danger"; but they admitted that the word *responsibility* "has been overworked and is unpopular . . ." Because of the overwhelming desire to stay out of war, probably only a small percentage of Americans in the mid-1930s would have agreed with Dulles's and Armstrong's contention that "we have the duty to support any reasonable move to organize the world more effectively for peace." [24]

Despite their determination to keep out of war, most Americans in the 1930s were developing increasingly hostile attitudes toward the three "dictator" nations which seemed to be threatening the peace. Animosity toward Japan was especially intense, but once favorable or at least ambivalent attitudes toward Germany and Italy also had been generally reversed by the mid-1930s.

In the 1920s, as we have seen, many Americans considered the Japanese people inferior and succeeded in having all Japanese immigration to the United States stopped. As early as the 1890s, American businessmen had feared Japanese economic competition, and after Japan's surprising victory over Russia in the Russo-Japanese War in the early 1900s, American strategists became concerned about Japan's potential as a military rival.

The image of the Japanese as tough competitors grew even

stronger during the depression. "Give a Japanese product an inch and it takes a mile," proclaimed the conservative *Saturday Evening Post* in 1934. Although the value of American exports to Japan exceeded the value of Japanese imports, cheap Japanese products were prominently displayed in chain stores, and some types of inexpensive cloth came primarily from Japan. Ignoring the favorable balance of trade, protectionists insisted that every Japanese-made pencil or toy forced another American worker onto the unemployment lines. With State Department assistance, some of the affected industries negotiated "gentlemen's agreements" with Japanese companies establishing voluntary quotas on exports to the United States.[25]

Favorable attitudes toward China also hurt Japan's image in the United States. For generations many Americans had experienced a love affair with China based as much on myths and selective perceptions as on realities. In contrast to the Japanese, the Chinese were not viewed as either economic or military competitors, but as simple peasants anxious to embrace Christianity and enjoy American products. American missionaries returned from China to tell congregations throughout the United States of the cooperative, educable Chinese, and American businessmen dreamed of a vast "China market" that would bring them wealth.

Children of American missionaries to China such as writer Pearl Buck and publisher Henry Luce, unlike any child of American missionaries to Japan, were able to add to the favorable picture of their childhood home. Buck's best-selling novel, *The Good Earth*, published in 1931 and made into a movie in 1936 seen by an estimated twenty-three million Americans, was the most famous of many books and articles giving a highly favorable portrayal of the Chinese people. Large numbers of pro-Chinese and anti-Japanese articles appeared throughout the 1930s in Luce's widely read publications, *Time, Life,* and *Fortune.*[26]

Japan's conquest of Manchuria beginning in September

1931, which fitted most newspaper editors' definition of front-page news, marked the first step in solidifying anti-Japanese attitudes. Some Americans sought to explain Japanese actions in Manchuria by insisting that they were little different from the frequent American military interventions in Latin America, but no one defended the bombing and shelling of Shanghai in January and February of 1932. Indiscriminate killing of civilians still was considered barbaric, and Americans had much closer ties with China than with Manchuria.

The attack on Shanghai sparked an intensive but short-lived movement to boycott all trade between the United States and Japan. The leader of the boycott effort was A. Lawrence Lowell, the nationally known president of Harvard University. Partially because of Lowell's leadership and contacts, the boycott movement was strongest on college campuses and in church and peace groups. Because Japan's actions were considered a moral outrage, a violation of the Kellogg-Briand Pact and other treaties of the 1920s, and a threat to the collective security principles of the League of Nations, both pacifists like Jane Addams and collective security internationalists like Raymond Buell could support an economic boycott. Newly formed organizations—the American Committee on the Far Eastern Crisis, the Emergency Peace Committee, and the American Boycott Association—argued that something had to be done to stop the Japanese and restore peace.[27]

Many others opposed a boycott. The *Washington Star*, for example, believed that a boycott would be a step toward war; its editors expressed surprise that peace groups would support a measure that might require "preparedness and determination to use the 'big stick.'" Some southern editors warned that a boycott would end the sale of cotton to Japan if, as seemed likely, Japan retaliated. The Scripps-Howard newspapers insisted that the United States should not impose a boycott alone, while the isolationist *Chicago Tribune* blamed China for being unprepared for the Japanese attack.[28]

Fortunately, tensions eased because the Japanese did not pursue a full-scale war against China in the early 1930s. But Americans, who had long considered themselves special friends and virtual protectors of the Chinese, neither forgave nor forgot Japanese behavior in Manchuria and China in the early 1930s.

Even before Japanese military actions in Manchuria and China, most Americans held much more favorable attitudes toward Germany than toward Japan. After World War I, Americans had quickly discarded their "Hun" image of Germany and had begun to adopt more favorable attitudes. German-Americans were a large and respected ethnic group, and their work in organizations like the Steuben Society of America emphasized the achievements of German culture and German-American contributions to American society. During the '1920s German diplomats, aware of the United States' economic power and its potential as a counterweight to France, cultivated friendly relations with the United States. By the late 1920s and early 1930s Americans generally were friendly toward Germany and sympathetic to German criticisms of the Versailles Treaty.[29]

The presence of Adolf Hitler's National Socialist Party on the German political scene made little impact on the American public. The American press tended to ridicule *Der Fuehrer* and belittle his chances of coming to power. But in January 1933, while the Japanese were extending their territory in northern China, Hitler became Chancellor of Germany.[30]

Although Germany in the early and mid-1930s was no military threat to the United States, Hitler's defiant nationalism and open anti-Semitism sparked considerable American concern. In the wake of acts against Jews in Germany, the American Jewish Committee, the American Jewish Congress, and B'nai B'rith sponsored an anti-Hitler rally in Madison Square Garden on March 27, 1933. Among those who addressed the overflow crowd were Senator Robert F. Wagner of New York, William Green, president of the American Federation of Labor, and Bishops William T. Manning of the Protestant Episcopal Church and Francis J. McConnell of the Methodist Episcopal Church. When overt anti-Semitism in Germany continued, Jewish leaders organized boycotts of German products. The two major organizations involved in developing the boycott—the Non-Sectarian Anti-Nazi League to Champion Human Rights and the Boycott Committee of the American Jewish Congress—were only partially successful in convincing Americans to carry out the boycott.[31]

The Roosevelt adminstration generally disapproved of anti-German activities. Unwilling to take a stand against Hitler, the administration tried to postpone the 1933 anti-Hitler rally and did little to help Jewish refugees from Germany. Not only was there considerable anti-Semitism in the United States in the 1930s, but there also was the problem of finding jobs for refugees at a time when ten million Americans were out of work. Trying to maintain normal relations with Germany, the State Department was embarrassed when a mock trial on "The Case of Civilization Against Hitlerism" attracted a large crowd to Madison Square Garden in March 1934 and when, after the Blood Purge of June 30–July 1, 1934, administration official Hugh Johnson said that recent events in Germany "made me sick . . ."[32]

According to a study of American newspaper coverage of Nazi Germany, the press, which occasionally had presented favorable stories in 1933 and early 1934, turned completely against Hitler after the purge. But because Hitler's behavior did not threaten other nations directly until the late 1930s, there was no clamor for actions stronger than boycotts against him.[33]

In 1935, as Benito Mussolini was announcing his designs on Ethiopia and Congress was passing neutrality legislation, attention shifted away from Germany and Japan and toward Italy. Americans generally had been favorable or at least ambivalent toward Italy during the thirteen years since Mussolini had risen to power. Newspaper and magazine coverage in the 1920s had been largely favorable toward Mussolini's corporate society, if not toward his possible goals in foreign policy, and during the early years of the depression Italy's booming economy looked like a possible model for the United States. Although labor unions and radicals never had liked Mussolini's Italy, many businessmen and conservative periodicals like the *Saturday Evening Post* consistently had praised the fascist regime. Many of the 4–5 million Italian-Americans also had been proud of Mussolini's leadership in the home country.[34]

When the Italo-Ethiopian War broke out in October 1935, many Italian-Americans strongly supported their former homeland. Large crowds turned out for pro-Mussolini rallies in northern cities, and gold wedding rings and watches as well as money were contributed to the cause. Organizations such as the American Friends of Italy, Sons of Italy, the American-Italian Union, and the newly formed League for American Neutrality sought to convince the public and policymakers of the justness of the Italian attack. Italian-American leaders were upset when the administration sought to prevent the shipment of supplies such as oil to Italy, and they also lobbied vigorously to ensure that the government did not join the League of Nations in seeking to apply effective sanctions against Italy.[35]

While most Italian-Americans apparently supported Mussolini, black Americans, many of whom had long considered Ethiopia to be the ancient center of black culture as well as its contemporary epitome, generally were outraged by the Italian invasion. Blacks purchased medical supplies for Ethiopia, organized boycotts of Italian-made goods, and demonstrated against Mussolini in Harlem and elsewhere. Harlem's *Amsterdam News* likened the Italian leader to "a mad dog running through a town." Walter White, executive director of the National Association for the Advancement of Colored People, said angrily that Italy "has set fire under the powder keg of white arrogance and greed which seems destined to become an act of suicide for the so-called white world." A prayer widely distributed to black houses of worship asked that God "grant no Ethiopian soldier misses when he fires and that every Italian bullet go astray." [36]

For the majority who had no strong ties with either Italy or Ethiopia, the Italian conquest of Ethiopia in 1935–36 shattered the generally favorable image of Mussolini that had developed over the past decade and placed Italy in the group of dangerous "dictator" nations. Even before the war began, Emperor Haile Selassie's dignified appeals to the League of Nations and to Washington swung opinion in favor of Ethiopia. The Italians might try to picture the Ethiopians as uncivilized, but there could be no doubt that Italy was the aggressor. When war broke out, angry crowds besieged the Italian consulate in San Francisco, 300 pro-Ethiopian demonstrators were arrested in Chicago, and a "Fair Play for Ethiopia" committee was organized in Brooklyn. Liberals, organized labor, and Protestants tended to condemn Mussolini more harshly than did conservatives, business spokesmen, and Catholics.[37]

President Roosevelt did not have to lead public opinion on this issue. Newspaper, radio, and especially newsreel coverage of Haile Selassie's appeal for assistance to the League of Nations and other dramatic events during the Italo-Ethiopian War added substantially to a powerful image being developed in the American consciousness during the 1930s. Most Americans might avoid thinking about possible implications, but the image was being embedded: the dictators were on the march.

3

THE IMPACT
OF WORLD WAR II,
1937–1945

One conception holds that the United States is morally responsible for the peace of Europe and the Orient, that only collective action can keep peace, that the President can always discover just who is an aggressor in any dispute, and that the United States cannot stay out of a general war if it comes. The other conception of policy denies these postulates. It holds that the United States does not have this moral responsibility and would not know how to exercise it if it did; that the one sure way to get into war is to takes sides in any dispute likely to lead to an open breach; that intervention[s] in disputes in Europe or the Orient are futile unless backed by a will to war in case of a major diplomatic defeat; and that the United States can and ought to stay out of European and Oriental wars, no matter what the pretexts on which they are started and waged.

—Charles Beard (1937) [1]

IN JULY 1937, when Japan initiated large-scale military action against China, the great majority of Americans believed, as did Professor Beard, that the highest priority of American foreign policy should be to keep out of war. Eight years later, when the Japanese sued for peace after the atomic attacks on Hiroshima and Nagasaki, an equally impressive majority supported the first set of assumptions in the above quotation. The transformation of American foreign policy during World War II involved the growth of a large national security bureaucracy, an increase in presidential power, and the stationing of American troops abroad. The basis for these changes was the transformation of American attitudes toward the proper role of the United States in world affairs.

A very large part of this shift in attitudes occurred during the four years and five months between the beginning of the major Japanese campaign against China and the attack at Pearl Harbor. During these years foreign policy issues dominated public discourse. Would the Loyalists be able to defeat the Nationalist challenge in Spain? Would Japan conquer China? Would Germany go to war with England and France? What was Russia's policy? Should the United States support England or remain neutral? Did Germany and Japan threaten the United States? What began in 1937 as divisiveness among the many publics gradually developed into something approaching a consensus on foreign policy issues even before Pearl Harbor.

One interpretation of the years leading up to Pearl Harbor holds that Roosevelt was indecisive and hesitant, that he overestimated the strength of noninterventionist sentiment, and that he failed to lead the nation toward more active resistance to the Axis powers as rapidly as public opinion actually would have permitted. While these charges may be partially valid for the period after the fall of France in June 1940, the fact is that Roosevelt had to move cautiously to allow time for the majority of both the mass and attentive publics to reach the conclusion that firmer steps to oppose Germany and Japan were justified. Roosevelt recognized the profound desire of most Americans to keep out of war, and he may also have understood better than some recent scholars the significance for foreign policy of the deep divisions within the public during these years.

By the late 1930s the combination of the Great Depression, the New Deal, and the succession of ominous events abroad had created divisions in American society and thought as pervasive and deeply rooted as any in recent American history. On the Left were the Communists, who were strong in some labor unions and among young people and intellectuals, plus socialists and other independent radicals. On the Right were those who advocated some form of fascism, plus the much larger number of businessmen and others who were determined to quash labor unions and "socialistic" New Deal legislation. So widely separated were the viewpoints that the liberals who supported the New Deal were considered lackeys of capitalism by the Left and softheaded idealists by the Right.

On domestic issues it is possible to make distinctions among those on the Left who wanted a socialist order or at least a greatly expanded New Deal, those in the middle who generally were pleased with the direction of Roosevelt's domestic policies, and those on the Right who considered the Wagner Labor Relations Act or the Social Security Act as a dangerous step toward socialism. But on foreign policy issues no such generalizations hold. Some conservatives, such as publisher Henry Luce, were interventionists (supporters of military aid to the Allies who accepted the possibility of American belligerency), while others, such as Robert McCormick, were noninterventionists (opponents of pro-Allied actions which might lead the United States into war). Liberals like Herbert Agar of the openly belligerent organization Fight for Freedom were strongly interventionist, while others like Frederick Libby of the National Council for the Prevention of War were fervently noninterventionist. And leftists like Socialist Party leader

Norman Thomas were noninterventionist, while the Communist Party vigorously followed the party line emanating from Moscow. Until the Nazi-Soviet Pact of August 1939, the Communists were among the most vocal advocates of collective security; from August 1939 until the German invasion of Russia in 1941, they carried noninterventionism to the point of leading strikes in war industries; and from June 1941 until Pearl Harbor, they championed American aid to embattled Russia and the other Allies.

Nor would Roosevelt have been encouraged to believe that the nation would become united behind a more forceful policy if he had shifted his focus from basic political orientation to ethnic affiliation. True, many Southerners and Northeasterners of English or Scotch-Irish descent supported more aid to the Allies, and so understandably did Jews shocked by Hitler's rabid anti-Semitism. But ethnic groups which held the balance of power in many of the large electoral states in the Northeast and Middle West—German-Americans, Irish-Americans, Italian-Americans, and others—tended to feel strongly that the United States should keep out of war.

An example of the serious divisions in public attitudes toward foreign policy in the late 1930s was the issue of American policy toward the Spanish civil war, which began in 1936 and which General Franco's Nationalists finally won in 1939. In early 1937 the United States imposed an embargo on shipments of arms to both sides. Because the effect of this policy was to favor Franco, and because the neutrality laws did not necessarily apply to civil wars, many liberals and radicals insisted that the United States should lift the embargo and permit shipments of arms to the Loyalists.

The controversy over lifting the embargo divided Left and Right, but it even more clearly revealed divisions between Catholics and Protestants. American Catholic leaders favored Franco and worked hard to retain the embargo. Not a single Catholic publication favored the Loyalists. When the issue of repeal came to a head in January 1939, Philadelphia Catholics alone sent ten thousand anti-repeal telegrams to Congress, and pro-embargo forces held a rally in Washington on January 9. When the pro-embargo forces won in Congress, angry liberals charged that the Catholic Church was pro-fascist.[2]

Divisions between Protestants and Catholics generally on this issue also are striking. A Gallup poll in December 1938 found that 83 percent of Protestants and 42 percent of Catholics who sympathized with one side or the other supported the Loyalists; conversely, 58 percent of Catholics and only 17 percent of Protestants supported Franco. A poll released a month later revealed that 20 percent of Catholics, 41 percent of Protestants, and 52 percent of Jews who had followed events in the civil war favored permitting the Loyalists to buy military supplies in the United States. Although the relative importance of the issue decreased, many Protestants and liberals continued to oppose conciliatory policies toward Spain as long as Franco remained in power.[3]

For Roosevelt, public opinion polls, notably the special polls and analyses Hadley Cantril of the Office of Public Opinion Research did for him, helped to keep him aware of these divisions and the inconsistencies of the public mind. Roosevelt "watched the fledgling polls," public opinion analyst Lloyd A. Free has noted, "and above all followed with avid interest data especially collected by my late colleague Hadley Cantril, charting trends in American opinion in connection with the war. With a close eye on Cantril's data, Roosevelt paced his course, escalating his effort to aid the British and defeat the Axis step by gradual step." [4]

The overwhelming majority of Americans consistently wanted to keep out of war, Cantril and other pollsters found, but growing majorities after 1939 also wanted to aid Britain and France, even if such aid increased the risk of war. Prohibit the sale of strategic goods to Japan, the public responded, but

1941: Aviation hero Charles A. Lindbergh (right) and Senator
Burton K. Wheeler (D., Montana) preached the "America First"
gospel.

don't send our boys overseas to die. Even more than usual, the results of public opinion polls in the years before Pearl Harbor seemed to turn on how the question was posed. To gauge the intensity with which opinions are held, a President may pay particular attention to the strength of the groups taking positions on an issue. One problem in using this technique in the Roosevelt years was that each group naturally claimed more public support than it could document. Another was that some groups peaked too early or too late: the Committee for Non-Participation in Japanese Aggression was founded in August 1938, well before most of the public was ready to accept serious actions against Japan; America First, the largest noninterventionist group, was formed in September 1940, well after the intensity of noninterventionist opinion had begun to decline. A third problem, as Manfred Jonas has pointed out, is that divisions among groups supporting a general perspective such as noninterventionism could be as large as divisions between groups supporting different perspectives. Some noninterventionists supported pacifism, for example, while others were nationalists who wanted high levels of military spending to develop a "fortress America." The more groups there are contesting an issue, an observer might well have concluded, the more they tend to cancel each other ·out.[5]

One must keep in mind for the entire period from 1937 to 1941 the multiplicity of perspectives from the American Council on Judaism to the German-American Bund and from Fight for Freedom to America First. But one can also observe that the attitudes of the majority of Americans who were not foreign policy activists generally were shaped less by the appeals of organizations and political leaders than by the course of events. As one historian concluded recently, "It was the crush of events which forced the nation to recognize its inevitable involvement in the world, the danger of continued isolation, and, finally, the necessity of war with the Axis." [6]

The period from the large-scale Japanese attack on China to Pearl Harbor can usefully be divided into three periods. The first of these, July 1937–August 1939, involved preparing for a new world war; the second, September 1939–June 1940, involved formally taking sides and concluding that the United States might be directly threatened; and the third, July 1940– December 1941, involved disregarding neutrality and expecting that the United States would be drawn into the war.

A clash between Chinese and Japanese troops on July 7, 1937, touched off sustained fighting which resulted in Japan's capturing most of China's cities and fertile farmlands in 1937 and 1938. Secretary of State Cordell Hull invoked principles of international morality against Japan in speeches in July and August 1937, and on October 5 in Chicago Roosevelt called on peace-loving nations to "quarantine" the aggressors "who are threatening a breakdown of all international order and law." Roosevelt never clarified precisely what steps he had in mind, and most historians now doubt that he was considering specific measures at the time. But the considerable press coverage given to the speech and to Roosevelt's additional comments about it made it clear that the administration's preoccupation with domestic affairs was past. [7]

On December 12, 1937, Japanese warplanes sank the U.S. gunboat *Panay* and damaged three Standard Oil Company tankers in the Yangtze River. Although Japanese leaders immediately apologized and agreed to pay indemnities, the incident provided dramatic headlines and added to the feeling that war was coming. A sailor aboard the *Panay* took motion pictures of the Japanese attack; the resulting footage was featured in newsreels in movie houses throughout the country, thus contributing to the image of the Japanese as enemies. In 1938 the administration's "moral embargo" effectively stopped the sale of airplanes to Japan. From 1938 through 1941, as the list of products which could not be sold to Japan gradually grew, Americans turned most of their attention to events in Europe.

Occupying center stage in Europe in 1938 and 1939 was Adolf Hitler, whose exploits many Americans followed closely. In March 1938 Austria was annexed to Germany, and soon thereafter Hitler turned his attention to Czechoslovakia, which had a large German minority in its westernmost section. When Hitler threatened war if the Sudetenland was not turned over to Germany by October 1, the French and British appealed for peace and agreed to meet Hitler at Munich on September 29 and 30. Despite the protests of the Czechoslovak government, Hitler received the Sudetenland in return for the promise that he would make no additional territorial demands in Europe. When Germany took over the remainder of Czechoslovakia the following spring and began making demands on Poland, the French and British made it clear that any attempt to dismember Poland would mean war.

The dramatic diplomatic events in Europe coincided with technical developments within American radio which allowed the networks to present up-to-the-minute reports from Europe, though not from Asia. And, as the extended coverage of the Munich conference showed, these broadcasts were quite popular. By bringing news from Europe daily to the living rooms of tens of millions of American families, the radio networks contributed profoundly not only to the expectation of war, but also to the sense that events in Europe unavoidably concerned Americans.

Despite Hitler's well-publicized successes, most Americans in 1938 and early 1939 believed that a major European war was not imminent. And even if war broke out, the public believed that the Allies would win and that the United States could remain neutral. In September 1938, for example, 86 percent said that England and France could defeat Germany in the event of war, and 57 percent said that the United States could keep out of such a war. As late as May 1939 only 32 percent of those with opinions believed that there would be a major European war that year. This configuration of generally optimistic attitudes toward events in Europe before September 1939 might be called confident noninterventionism.[8]

Although most Americans in the late 1930s believed that the United States would be able to keep out of war, large majorities supported increased defense expenditures. At the end of 1937, 69 percent believed that the United States should enlarge the army, 74 percent approved a larger navy, and 80 percent supported an enlarged air force. Eleven months later, after the Czechoslovakian crisis had dramatized the danger of war in Europe, the already impressive majorities had grown to 82 percent for a larger army, 86 percent for a larger navy, and 90 percent for a larger air force.[9]

Finally, American opinion of Germany plummeted during 1938. The public considered the Czechoslovakian crisis and Nazi persecutions of Jews and Catholics as the two "most interesting" news stories of 1938; they also were the most ominous. Seventy-seven percent of those with opinions believed that Germany's demand for the annexation of the Sudetenland was unjustified, and 60 percent believed that the Munich agreements increased the likelihood of war. When asked in October 1938 whether they believed Hitler's statement that he had no more territorial ambitions in Europe, 92 percent said, "No." And 61 percent—including 96 percent of Jewish respondents—said that they would "join a movement in this country to stop buying German-made goods."[10]

The crucial changes in attitudes toward involvement in World War II occurred between September 1, 1939, when Germany invaded Poland, and June 20, 1940, when France agreed to an armistice with Germany. The outbreak of war in Europe led to revision of America's neutrality laws, thus signaling that the dominance of the noninterventionist viewpoint had ended. Despite warnings from noninterventionists that aid to the Allies eventually would draw the United States into the second European war in a generation, England and

Frankie and Johnnie

June 1940: Neutrality laws still hampered FDR as the Battle of Britain began, but public opinion was turning pro-British.

Editorial cartoon by Dan Dowling. Reproduced through the courtesy of Field Newspaper Syndicate

France now would be able to buy munitions in the United States. In the spring of 1940, when the German *blitzkrieg* conquered France and all countries to the north, most Americans moved toward the conclusion that defeating Hitler was a more important goal than staying out of war. Once the public reached that conclusion and became psychologically prepared for war, the administration could become more forthright in its support for the Allies in Europe and in its hostility toward Japan.

Historians who have applauded the revision of the neutrality laws and other steps toward direct American involvement in World War II have given considerable credit to the work of William Allen White's Non-Partisan Committee for Peace through Revision of the Neutrality Act in the fall of 1939 and to the work of his Committee to Defend America by Aiding the Allies beginning in May 1940. These organizations, benefiting from Roosevelt's personal support, did mobilize effectively the support that was developing for a more interventionist course. But it must be emphasized again that pro-Allied attitudes themselves were influenced less by organizations than by the events in Europe and Asia and by the way in which those events were presented in the most influential media.

What was especially unsettling about events in Europe was not that the Germans could defeat Poland or Denmark or even France, but that each of these countries fell so rapidly. Between September 1939 and June 1940 the Germans made conquest look easy. If the Germans could defeat small nations in weeks and France in less than two months, how long would it take for Hitler to conquer England and Russia before confronting the last remaining hostile power, the United States? And would not Japan seek to emulate Hitler's European successes in Asia, thus leaving the United States isolated and vulnerable on both flanks?

White's committees and Roosevelt received invaluable assistance from the mass media in propagating such frightening perspectives. The Luce periodicals were at the height of their influence, and virtually every issue of *Time* and *Life* featured stories on Europe which were strongly pro-British and anti-German and stories on Asia which were even more strongly pro-Chinese and anti-Japanese. The major radio networks, National Broadcasting Company and Columbia Broadcasting System, also were strongly favorable to the Allies. The British Broadcasting Corporation provided commentaries on public affairs, speeches by Prime Minister Winston Churchill, and other material which was broadcast on American networks. Edward R. Murrow and other American correspondents in London and elsewhere in Europe provided vivid reports on the experience of the war for civilians as well as soldiers, and popular commentators such as Raymond Gram Swing and H. V. Kaltenborn supported the interventionist position. Newsreels such as "The March of Time" frequently ridiculed Hitler and other Axis leaders, and gave the impression that Japan was determined to conquer India and Australia as well as China and Southeast Asia. Newspapers were more divided between noninterventionist and interventionist perspectives, but the press's emphasis on violence and on sensational charges also fostered the growth of a wartime psychology. Mass opinion shifted in 1939 and 1940 in the wake of dramatic events dramatically presented. The outbreak of war in September 1939 resulted in a substantial shift in opinion on the question which probably provided the best gauge of interventionist versus noninterventionist opinion. In the spring of 1939, when general war seemed unlikely, only 31 percent of those with opinions believed that the United States should sell munitions to England and France. At the time of the Nazi-Soviet pact in late August, when war seemed imminent, support had risen to 50 percent. By mid-September the percentage stood at 57, and by late September, after Roosevelt's address to Congress calling for revision of the neutrality laws, it had climbed to 62 percent. Although the percentage dropped to 56 in late October after the noninterventionists had organized opposition to the administration's proposals, a majority of the public clearly supported the Neutrality Act which Roosevelt signed into law on November 4, 1939.[11]

During the "phony war" between Hitler's fall 1939 and spring 1940 offensives, Joseph Stalin dealt another blow to the noninterventionist cause. After the Finnish government refused to accede to Stalin's territorial demands, Russian troops invaded Finland on November 30, 1939. For once, public opinion was virtually unanimous: the Russian invasion was an outrage against civilization, and interventionists and noninterventionists alike rushed to provide humanitarian relief to the Finns. The intensity of opinion against Russia was stronger than it had been against Germany three months before. Anglophiles joined Anglophiles in denouncing Russia, and conservatives saw an opportunity to discredit American Communists. By the time Finland sued for peace in March 1940, the policy of remaining aloof from Europe's turmoil seemed less and less desirable.

Hitler's spring offensive beginning April 9, 1940, dealt the decisive blow to noninterventionism. By June public support had increased sharply for instituting a draft, for strengthening national defense, for increasing military aid to England, and for nominating presidential candidates who would put aid to England above keeping the nation out of war. In early May, 55 percent believed that the Allies would win the war, 17 percent believed that Germany would win, and 28 percent expressed no opinion. By late June, after the fall of France, the percentage which believed that Germany would win had doubled to 35, the percentage which believed that the Allies would win had dropped to 32, and 33 percent expressed no opinion. Because most Americans believed that a Germany triumphant in Europe would attack the United States, many had concluded that the United States would have to fight Hitler sooner or later. Why not, therefore, support the position of the Committee to Defend America by Aiding the Allies that the United States should give all possible aid to Britain in the hope that, as long as Britain remained in the war, the United States could keep out? [12]

Hitler's spring offensive also led to a rise in the number of Americans who were ready for the United States to declare war immediately without being attacked. In mid-May only 7 percent favored such a course, but by late June the percentage had doubled to 14. The change represented an increase of several million adult Americans who now held an opinion well in advance of official policy. In early June, as if sensing this movement of opinion, a group of prominent interventionists issued a press release in which they called upon the government to confront the "logic of the situation" and declare war on Germany. Although most Americans continued until Pearl Harbor to oppose such a step, the public after June 1940 generally supported anti-Axis actions which clearly could lead to war.[13]

In retrospect, the final sixteen months before Pearl Harbor appear to have been a time of waiting for the United States to be drawn into full belligerency. By the summer of 1940 the

United States was already the "arsenal of democracy" for Great Britain and China to the extent that it had destroyers and other implements of war to spare; the passage of Lend-Lease in March 1941 meant that the Allies would be given what they usually had paid for in the past. The percentage of Americans who said they would vote to enter the war immediately never rose more than ten points above the 14 percent of June 1940, and usually hovered around 20 percent. But the belief that the United States inevitably would enter the war—what one contemporary observer called the "coefficient of fatalism"—grew from 51 percent in May 1940 to 59 percent in December 1940 to 82 percent in April 1941. When the Gallup organization later that month again asked whether the United States would enter the war, 13 percent replied that "we are already in"! [14]

After June 1940 the public consistently put more emphasis on anti-Axis actions than on keeping out of the war. Sixty percent of those with opinions in December 1940 put helping England above keeping out of war; 70 percent in August 1941 agreed that the United States should "take steps now to keep Japan from becoming more powerful, even if it means risking a war with Japan"; and 68 percent in November 1941 believed that defeating Germany was more important than keeping out of war. A subtle but important shift is apparent: the emphasis on "helping England," which dominated from the fall of France to the passage of Lend-Lease, gave way by the fall of 1941 to emphasis on defeating the Axis powers. Unfortunately for the Japanese, their attack on Pearl Harbor coincided with the full readiness for war of the vast majority of the American people. [15]

Many Americans who lived during World War II have tended to romanticize that era. Books, movies, and records dealing with the war frequently have sold well, and many Americans have idolized such military leaders of the period as Patton, MacArthur, and Eisenhower. World War II apparently stands for many Americans as a time when the nation was united in support of a totally just cause. Largely forgotten are the wartime complaints about profiteering, the black market, unequal sacrifices, bureaucratic red tape, and untrustworthy allies.

It is true that the vast majority of Americans supported the war effort after Pearl Harbor and continued to support necessary sacrifices until unconditional surrender was achieved. But while the fundamental divisions between interventionists and noninterventionists on whether to enter the war had been resolved, there were still strong differences of opinion on foreign policy between nationalists and collective security internationalists. There also were significant differences in outlook toward the principal enemies, Germany and Japan, and toward the principal allies, Great Britain, China, and Russia.

Most Americans believed that the war was being fought against Germany's Nazi leadership, not against the German people. When the Gallup organization asked in November 1942, "In the war with Germany, do you feel that our chief enemy is the German people as a whole, or the German government?", 74 percent answered German government while 6 percent said German people. When the National Opinion Research Center asked that same fall whether "the German people should be blamed for the cruelties to religious groups, the mass killings in occupied countries, and the tortures in concentration camps," 60 percent said, "No." Because many Americans were of German descent, because cultural ties with Germany were strong, and because the government did not encourage anti-German attitudes to the extent that it had in World War I, there was little hatred of the German people during the war.[16]

By contrast, hatred of Germany's leaders was pronounced. When asked, "What do you think should be done with the Nazi leaders after the war?", a plurality of 35 percent said, "Hang or shoot," and others wanted them tortured slowly or treated "as Nazis have treated others." A San Francisco teacher wanted Hitler put in a prison cell and forced to listen to recordings of his own speeches until he lost his sanity.[17]

As for treatment of Germany after the war, most wanted American troops left there for several years to eradicate Nazism and prevent Germany from planning another war. There was more sentiment for destroying Germany's industrial base and making it primarily agricultural among the less well educated than among the college educated, but majority opinion among all groups in February 1945 was for "close supervision and control." [18]

Animosity toward the "sneaky Japs" who had attacked Pearl Harbor ran much deeper. "The fact that we were pushed around by a slant-eyed people to whom we feel racially superior, is an important element in the rage against Japan," public opinion analyst William A. Lydgate wrote in 1944. Such words as *bestial, sadistic, dirty, barbaric,* and *treacherous,* not to mention expletives, were part of the vocabulary used to discuss the Japanese. In one public opinion poll, complete extermination was favored five times as frequently for the Japanese as for the Germans. As a Dallas housewife put it: "Annihilate the whole Japanese race. Get rid of the last one, women and children too." Although the majority did not hold such extreme views, anti-Japanese feeling was strong, especially among the less well educated.[19]

Hatred of the Japanese—including, especially on the West Coast, Japanese-Americans—carried over into substantial support for using weapons which annihilated civilians and imposing a harsh peace. In December 1944, 43 percent favored the use of poison gas against Japanese cities and, immediately after the attacks on Hiroshima and Nagasaki, 85 percent approved "using the new atomic bomb on Japanese cities." When asked in November 1944 what the United States should do with Japan after the war, a plurality of 33 percent believed that it should be destroyed as a political entity, and an ad-

1942: President Roosevelt's pledge to carry war to the Japanese was applauded by a public outraged at the Pearl Harbor attack.

ditional 13 percent suggested killing all the Japanese people. Attitudes had moderated in the direction of strict control and reeducation by late July 1945.[20]

Why were hostile feelings toward Japan so intense? The attack on Pearl Harbor, feelings of racial superiority, distrust of Japanese-Americans, contempt for Japanese fighting tactics —all surely played a part. But ignorance of Japan and its cultural heritage also helps to explain why many Americans hated Japan but not Germany. Japanese history was not taught in the schools and cultural developments were not discussed in the mass media or the pulpit. Despite three years of well-publicized war in the Far East, in May 1945 fewer than one-third of Gallup's respondents could locate on a map Guam, Okinawa, Java, or Singapore, and fewer than one-half could locate Osaka and Kyushu. During World War II and subsequent Asian wars, the Far East was foreign to most Americans in ways that Europe was not.[21]

Great Britain, the nation with which Americans had the closest cultural ties, also was the most popular. British opposition to Germany in the spring of 1940, the dramatic rescue of British soldiers at Dunkirk, and the air war over Britain later that year enhanced Britain's standing in the United States. Eloquent, colorful Winston Churchill gave speeches which were carried on American radio and made frequent visits to the United States throughout the war. Churchill was so popular that even his opposition to independence for India did little to diminish his stature. Americans during World War II tended to dislike European colonialism, but they admired and felt kinship toward the British people.

Opinion polls confirmed Britain's premier position. In August 1943, 61 percent of all respondents favored a permanent military alliance with Britain after the war; 56 percent were willing to make such an alliance with China, and 39 percent with Russia. In a *Fortune* poll in early 1944, 72 percent wanted Britain to join the United States in forming a new international organization, while 67 and 65 percent wanted

China and Russia respectively to be founders of the organization. When asked, "Which of these countries would you want to have the most say?", 85 percent answered Great Britain, 72 percent said Russia, and 63 percent said China.[22]

As indicated in these and other polls, China remained the second most popular foreign nation among the mass public. Chiang Kai-shek and Madame Chiang received highly favorable coverage in the Luce periodicals, in the widely circulated *Reader's Digest,* and in the nationalistic press. Most Americans apparently assumed that the Chinese were doing all they could to defeat the common enemy, Japan. But a growing number of books and articles directed at the attentive public were sharply critical of Chiang's regime, which was charged with pervasive corruption and inefficiency. The informality and egalitarianism of the Chinese Communists impressed American visitors to Communist-controlled areas; many came to believe that Mao Tse-tung and his supporters might prove to be better rulers of China than the Nationalist regime. So much else was occurring in the world, however, that most Americans readily could ignore the continuing civil war inside China. [23]

When the Germans invaded Russia on June 22, 1941, the major war news shifted from Britain to Hitler's eastern front. If Hitler could defeat Russia and seize her oil and other resources, many American commentators believed that he would be virtually unbeatable. But if Russia held, the Germans would be caught in a dreaded two-front war in which the odds clearly would favor the Allies.

Winston Churchill once described Russia as a mystery wrapped inside an enigma. But to Americans of the 1930s and 1940s, who tended to believe what was convenient to believe about Russia as well as China, Russia might best be called a surprise. Russia sought alliances with the West against Hitler, yet signed a nonaggression pact with Germany in August 1939. When Hitler invaded Russia less than two years later, most American observers, impressed by Germany's quick win over France and Russia's apparent backwardness, believed that Germany would win within a few months. Yet Russia held and broke German offensive strength at Stalingrad in the fall of 1942. When Stalin met with Hull at Moscow and Roosevelt at Teheran in the fall of 1943, most Americans believed that Russia and the United States would continue to cooperate for world peace after the war was over. Yet serious and increasingly visible differences divided the allies well before Japan was defeated.

Within two years after the German invasion of Russia, American opinion generally had shifted from strong suspicion of Russia to gratitude for the Russian contribution to victory and confidence in the future of Soviet-American relations. Events in the Russo-German war, administration efforts to win public support for Russia as an ally, and favorable coverage in the media contributed most to the reversal of attitudes. Roosevelt, for example, frequently praised the Russian war effort; he also asked the head of Warner Brothers to make a film version of Joseph Davies's best-selling pro-Russian book, *Mission to Moscow*. Henry Luce devoted a special issue of *Life* in March 1943 to improvements in Russian living conditions under Lenin and Stalin. But the most important factor was that, at great cost to themselves, Russians were killing German soldiers and pointing the way toward eventual victory.

The pro-Russian majority generally did not recognize the fortuitous combination of circumstances—a war for survival, favorable administration policy, general reluctance of former noninterventionists to question official policy—upon which the favorable attitudes toward Russia rested. The majority also found it easy to ignore those who continued to be profoundly suspicious of Stalin—scattered intellectuals like William Henry Chamberlin and Max Eastman, most of the Catholic hierarchy, many Americans of East European descent, and right-wing nationalists who always had disliked Communism more than National Socialism. When by late 1944 or early

1945 many Americans began to fear Russian domination of Eastern Europe more than they appreciated Russia's continuing contribution to victory, the eventual collapse of the pro-Russian majority was foreseeable.[24]

Of more lasting significance than wartime attitudes toward the major enemies and allies was the growth during World War II of both internationalism and nationalism. Many of the former collective security internationalists and pacifists put their faith in a new international organization with sufficient power to maintain peace. Fervent nationalists such as Senator Robert Reynolds of North Carolina and newspaper magnate William Randolph Hearst wanted the United States to possess the military strength to maintain peace by itself. Most Americans, including powerful Republican Senator Arthur H. Vandenberg of Michigan, were in between, their ideas influenced by both the need for collective security and the belief that American ideals and power should prevail in the postwar world. The attack on Pearl Harbor, Vandenberg wrote later, "ended isolationism for any realist." But neither Pearl Harbor nor the remainder of World War II fully clarified just what should replace it.[25]

By 1943 collective security internationalists and pacifists were working to ensure that Allied victory in World War II would result in a lasting peace. Many believed that if the United States had joined the League of Nations and worked diligently for its success, World War II would have been averted. Only American leadership in a new world organization, therefore, could prevent an even more horrible World War III.

New peace groups sprouted like mushrooms and old ones were rejuvenated. In 1943 the League of Nations Association transformed itself into the United Nations Association. Also very active in building support for international organization were the Commission to Study the Organization of Peace, the Foreign Policy Association, the Non-Partisan Council to Win the Peace, and the Women's Action Committee for Victory and Lasting Peace, which included representatives from the American Association of University Women, the General Federation of Women's Clubs, the League of Women Voters, and other national women's organizations. As they had during the League of Nations controversy, Protestants in such organizations as the Federal Council of Churches played a major role in building support for international organization. Presbyterian layman John Foster Dulles first came to national prominence as head of the Federal Council of Churches' Commission to Study the Bases of a Just and Durable Peace. "The sovereignty system is no longer consonant either with peace or with justice," Dulles declared in 1941. "It is imperative that there be transition to a new order." Tens of thousands of foreign policy activists worked during the remainder of the war to translate such sentiments into functioning institutions.[26]

Many government officials also worked to prepare public opinion for American leadership in a new world organization. Remembering Wilson's defeat, Roosevelt avoided personal leadership on this issue, but Vice President Henry A. Wallace strongly supported the internationalist cause. Resolutions favoring American membership in a new international organization passed in both the House of Representatives and the Senate in 1943 by margins of more than ten to one. Bipartisan teams of Congressmen made well-publicized speaking tours in support of American leadership in establishing institutions to maintain peace. And the Department of State's Office of Public Affairs, in cooperation with the Office of War Information, made and distributed pamphlets, films, radio programs, and other pro-United Nations materials to build public support for international organization. This effective "public-relations blitzkrieg" was the forerunner of information campaigns by executive agencies in the postwar period designed to build support for such policies as the Marshall Plan and American intervention in Vietnam.[27]

Supporters of international organization appeared to have

the mass public on their side throughout the war. The National Opinion Research Center asked on four separate occasions, "If a union of nations is formed after the war, do you think it would be a good or bad idea for the United States to join it?" The percentage responding "good idea" was 68 in September 1942, 70 in January and June 1943, and 71 in February 1944. The response to similar questions asked by the Gallup organization was 73 percent favorable in June 1942 and 72 percent favorable in June 1944. When Gallup asked in March 1945, "Do you think the United States should join a world organization with police power to maintain world peace?", 81 percent said, "Yes," 11 percent said, "No," and 8 percent had no opinion. In response to the next question in the same poll, 83 percent said that it was "very important" that the United States join such a world organization.[28]

Although such figures are impressive, one must remember that support for a general concept to be implemented in the future is quite different from wholehearted support of an existing imperfect institution. And questions which asked what sacrifices Americans would be willing to accept to support an international organization showed much lower levels of public approval. When asked in 1943 if they would support international organization even if the allies would owe nothing for Lend-Lease and the enemies would not be expected to pay any reparations, or if foreign goods were allowed to undersell American products in the United States, or if American armed forces were disbanded while other nations did the same, the majority of the public no longer favored American membership in an international organization. What the public generally seemed to want was an effective international organization and, at the same time, no diminution of American sovereignty.[29]

During World War II many observers were impressed by the shift in public attitudes from the noninterventionism of the 1930s to the conviction that the United States had to be willing to form alliances and join an international organization to preserve peace. In emphasizing these changes, wartime public opinion analysts tended to overlook the elements of continuity in public attitudes toward world affairs, notably the belief in what John Morton Blum recently called "the special virtue of the American experiment and those participating in it." When one examines editorials, speeches, advertisements, movies, diaries, and other documents from the World War II period, one is impressed repeatedly by the strength of nationalistic sentiments in America at that time.[30]

Feelings of national superiority among the mass public were revealed dramatically in a 1942 poll. Respondents were given a list of seventeen nationalities or races and asked to rate them in comparison with Americans. Only the first five were considered by a majority (ranging from 76 percent for Canadians to 56 percent for Irish) as being "as good as we are in all important respects":

1. Canadians	10. Jewish refugees
2. English	11. Poles
3. Dutch	12. Russians
4. Scandinavians	13. Chinese
5. Irish	14. Spaniards
6. French	15. Italians
7. Germans	16. Mexicans
8. Greeks	17. Japanese
9. South Americans	

It should be noted that the top seven, including the five groups whom the majority considered equal to Americans, all shared with most Americans a northern European background.[31]

Or consider responses to Gallup's question in June 1943, "Which of these countries do you think has done the most toward winning the war so far—Russia, China, Britain, or the United States?" Fifty percent of Britons said Russia, 42 percent said Britain, 5 percent said China, and 3 percent said the United States. Fifty-five percent of Americans chose the United States, 32 percent chose Russia, 9 percent chose

Britain, and 4 percent chose China. Britons probably over-estimated their own nation's contribution and underestimated the American contribution. But at a time when Russia and Britain had done most of the fighting in Europe, and China had done most of the fighting in Asia, it is suggestive of the strength of nationalistic sentiment that more than half of the American respondents chose the United States.[32]

During World War II nationalistic attitudes were strongest among conservative Republicans, members of patriotic and veterans organizations, and those with less than a high school education—in short, among prewar nationalistic noninterventionists who remained suspicious of alliances and international organization. Recognizing that efforts to isolate America from world problems had failed, the nationalists wanted the United States to become militarily superior to any possible combination of enemies. Whereas the fervent internationalists hoped that the United Nations would maintain peace and prevent a postwar armaments race, the fervent nationalists wanted American power to be the final arbiter of world affairs.

In its more moderate and widely shared formulation, nationalism as applied to foreign policy meant that American policies and ideals should prevail because they were morally right. The United States had no selfish motives in world affairs; what it advocated was for the good of mankind. "Because America alone among the nations of the earth was founded on ideas and ideals which transcend class and caste and racial and occupational differences," Henry Luce wrote in 1942, "America alone can provide the pattern of the future." The United States, Roosevelt and Hull insisted repeatedly, was fighting for the noble principles contained in the Atlantic Charter and Roosevelt's Four Freedoms address. When Hull addressed Congress in November 1943 after attending the Moscow Conference, he reported that, because other nations accepted American ideals, "there will no longer be need for spheres of influence, for alliances, for balance of power, or any other of the special arrangements through which, in the unhappy past, the nations strove to safeguard their security or to promote their interests." [33]

In the optimistic mood of 1943, Congressmen applauded Hull's speech and the public approved the apparent accomplishments of the Moscow Conference. The public also was heartened by the apparent success of the Yalta Conference in February 1945 in restoring Allied unity. Echoing Hull's idealistic remarks sixteen months earlier, Roosevelt reported to Congress in March 1945 that the agreements at Yalta "ought to spell the end of the system of unilateral action, the exclusive alliances, the spheres of influence, the balances of power, and all the other expedients that have been tried for centuries—and have always failed." But the American people learned quickly after the end of World War II that alliances and other diplomatic arrangements were as important as ever, and they also began to realize that other nations did not necessarily accept American ideals. [34]

4

ANXIETY AND ANTI-COMMUNISM, 1946–1962

The way I feel, I think what's happening in the world right now is pretty serious. Sometimes you go to bed, and you don't *know* when you go to bed if you're going to wake up; you might be blown off the earth while you're still sleeping! You're living in the Atomic Age today. Seven or eight thousand miles don't mean anything. The fast planes—jet planes, thunderbolts, rockets—they're building them nowadays to *travel*. How do we know when we go to bed, or in the day when we're working, what will happen?

—black man living in a northeastern city, interviewed in October 1950 for the Survey Research Center.[1]

BETWEEN THE END of World War II in August 1945 and the Cuban missile crisis in October 1962, the United States experienced generally increasing prosperity at home and unprecedented economic and military power abroad. But America's preeminent position in world affairs, together with the new danger of nuclear war and a bitter rivalry with the Soviet

Union, was more a source of anxiety than of satisfaction for most Americans.

The strong feelings of anxiety in the United States beginning in the mid-1940s had diverse roots. Concern about a depression once war orders ceased, about jobs for millions of veterans, about inflation as price controls were lifted, about strikes in industries in which the end of war-related overtime shrank paychecks, about whether women should leave the job market and return to the kitchen—these and other issues growing out of the dislocations of World War II and its aftermath contributed to the dissatisfaction which was reflected in the Republican campaign slogan of 1946, "Had enough?" The victory over Germany and Japan and the founding of the United Nations were supposed to relegate international relations to relative obscurity. But the failure of the United Nations to resolve the most important international issues, the arrival of the frightening atomic era, and serious disagreements with Russia contributed to the feeling that victory over the Axis powers had brought problems instead of peace.

The events and public debate from 1937 through 1941 assured that the United States would become interventionist in foreign affairs, but the form American peacetime involvement would take remained nebulous throughout the war. What became clear soon after the war was the hold which the Munich analogy had on the thinking of President Truman and many other Americans. According to this analogy, Stalin had replaced Hitler as the dictator seeking world domination. If the United States in dealing with Russia avoided the appeasement which had abetted Hitler's aggression in the late 1930s, then Communism could be contained and World War III could be averted.[2]

During the Truman, Eisenhower, and Kennedy years, the executive branch had an unusually large influence on public thinking about foreign affairs. The public information divisions of the State Department, the Defense Department, the White House, and other executive agencies—much larger and more sophisticated than during the 1920s and 1930s—were able to convey the administration's viewpoint and to withhold information which might support opposing viewpoints. Members of Congress—even those on important committees dealing with foreign policy issues—frequently believed that they lacked the expertise and information necessary to challenge national security decisions. Many journalists and scholars also assumed that it was patriotic as well as practical not to question too sharply the rationales for particular policies. Proud of their nation's role in defeating the Axis powers and in providing leadership of the "Free World" against Communism, most Americans looked to the President and other administration officials for guidance on foreign policy issues.

The years from 1946 through 1952, the years in which the Cold War consensus on American foreign policy was established, were a time of constant and disturbing change in foreign affairs. These also were the years in which the major features of the world as it would be known a generation later took shape. Communist governments gradually were established in the areas in Eastern Europe and the Far East occupied by Russian armies during World War II. Capitalistic societies grew in strength in the areas of Western Europe and the Far East occupied by American armies. India and other colonies won independence in the late 1940s, and European colonialism elsewhere in Asia, Africa, and Latin America clearly was doomed. Despite Arab hostility, Israel in 1948 became a nation, gained official American support, and expanded its territory for the first time. That same year Yugoslavia became the first Communist nation to break with Moscow. In 1949 the Soviet Union exploded an atomic bomb, thus ending the American monopoly, and the Communists finally won the civil war in China. In order to prevent the spread of Communism in Asia, the United States in 1950 intervened directly in a war in Korea and sent munitions to the French for use in Indochina. And the proliferation of nuclear weapons moved a step further when Britain exploded its first bomb in 1952.

How did the public generally respond to these and to such other significant developments as the use of billions of dollars to bolster European economic and military strength? Because of general acceptance of the premise of world leadership that grew out of the wartime experience, and because of the widespread fear of Russia and Communism that developed during the eighteen months after the Japanese surrender, most Americans—notably those with college educations and knowledge of specific issues—supported whatever policies the Truman administration considered necessary to combat Communism. Only when the Korean War turned into a stalemate involving increased American casualties did the majority begin to question the wisdom of this particular anti-Communist policy.

At the end of World War II many Americans, anxious to turn their attention to domestic affairs, hoped that the United Nations would be able to resolve international disputes and maintain peace. If the polls are accurate, the overwhelming majority of the public in the late 1940s and early 1950s wanted the United Nations strengthened and believed that it was "very important" that the United States work to make the world body a success. But as relations between the United States and Russia deteriorated, increasing numbers of Americans became dissatisfied with the U.N.'s performance. Whereas 37 percent were satisfied and 37 percent were dissatisfied with the U.N.'s performance in April 1946, only 21 percent were satisfied and 54 percent were dissatisfied two years later. Because most Americans believed that the U.N.'s main function was to preserve peace, it is not surprising that the percentage of those satisfied with the U.N.'s performance fell even lower during the Korean War.[3]

The United Nations also was viewed as a possible means of controlling atomic weapons. Although some liberals, religious leaders, and atomic scientists had criticized the use of atomic weapons against Japanese cities, most Americans had supported Truman's decision and rejoiced that the war was over. But the mind-boggling new weapons raised persistent questions. Should control of atomic energy be turned over to an international agency? Should the United States continue to test and manufacture atomic weapons? Should the United States keep the secret or share it with Russia and other nations? How soon would other nations develop the bomb? Were spies giving the formula to Russia? Did atomic weapons increase or decrease the likelihood of war?

The college-educated were the most favorable in 1945 and 1946 to international control of atomic energy, and they also were the most willing in 1948 to permit U.N. inspection of atomic installations in the United States as part of a plan to control atomic energy. But the college-educated were less willing than others to renounce the first use of atomic weapons in warfare. Only 18 percent of the college group, 19 percent of the high school group, and 22 percent of the grade school group in July 1949 supported such a pledge. Atomic weapons and American leadership in atomic technology were considered America's trump card: in early 1950, for example, the public favored development of the hydrogen bomb by a margin of more than four to one.[4]

One reason why the public supported the development of nuclear weapons clearly was fear of Russia and the desire to remain ahead of the Russians militarily. By the late 1940s opposition to Russia was the main rationale for most aspects of American foreign policy: increased military spending, the formation of alliances, economic and military aid, and possible rearmament of West Germany and Japan, among others. Opposition to Russia also provided the rationale, especially welcome to conservatives, for restricting the civil liberties of American Communists and purported fellow-travelers and for discrediting supporters of liberal causes generally.

Despite the generally favorable wartime attitudes, wide-

1948: The public now saw Russia as dangerously aggressive, and many called for an even tougher policy by President Truman.

Hutton in the *Philadelphia Inquirer*

spread public animosity toward Russia developed quickly after the war. Nourished by many politicians of both parties, by large segments of the mass media and the religious press, and by negative interpretations of Russian actions in Eastern Europe, Iran, and elsewhere, public attitudes were highly unfavorable as early as 1946. By March 1946 only 7 percent of Gallup's sample approved of "the policy Russia is following in world affairs." Two months later 58 percent responded that "Russia is trying to build herself up to be the ruling power of the world," while only 29 percent chose the more favorable view that Russia is "just building up protection against being attacked in another war." By October 1947 the percentage choosing "ruling power" had risen to 76 and the percentage choosing "protection" had dropped to 18. The Survey Research Center reported in late 1948 an "almost unanimous belief that Russia is an aggressive, expansion-minded nation."[5]

As Stalin in 1948 tightened his grip on Eastern Europe and threatened the Western position in Berlin, both belligerent attitudes toward Russia and the expectation of war increased. When Gallup in March 1948 asked the open-ended question, "What policy do you think we should follow toward Russia?", a plurality responded "prepare to fight, build up armed forces." The other most frequent responses were "be firm, no appeasement" and "go to war." Fewer than 5 percent suggested conciliatory steps like "get together, work things out" or "let U.N. work things out." Seventy-three percent of the same sample said that the United States was "too soft" in its policy toward Russia. In August 1948, 57 percent believed that there would be another major war within ten years, and 32 percent believed that the United States would be at war within a year.[6]

In light of the hardening views toward Russia, it is not surprising that Americans in the late 1940s supported increased military expenditures and a year of compulsory military service for all young men, a proposal commonly known as universal military training. More than two-thirds of those with opinions in February 1948 and in January 1949 supported an enlarged army, navy, and air force, and substantial majorities also were willing to pay higher taxes to support the military. Although more than 70 percent of the public consistently supported Truman's proposal for universal military training, the measure was delayed and then defeated in Congress largely because of concern about substantially increased costs and persistent lobbying by church, labor, and peace groups.[7]

But the intense bipartisan hostility toward Russia did make possible the passage of Truman's three most significant initiatives in foreign policy: aid to Greece and Turkey in 1947, the Marshall Plan for economic aid to Western Europe in 1948, and American leadership in establishing the North Atlantic Treaty Organization (NATO) as a formal military alliance in 1949. Mounting large public relations campaigns and supporting private groups such as the Citizens Committee for the Marshall Plan, the administration carefully built public and bipartisan Congressional support before bringing these measures to a vote. In 1947, the public was much more favorable to economic than to military aid to Greece and Turkey; by 1949 the public, increasingly perceiving the Communist threat as primarily military, strongly supported both economic and military aid.[8]

Although majorities approved all three of these programs, support consistently was highest among the college-educated, who also were the best informed about these as well as other foreign policy issues. Asked shortly after the Truman Doctrine speech in March 1947 whether they approved of $250 million in aid to Greece, 65 percent of the college group, 57 percent of the high school group, and 48 percent of the grade school group said, "Yes." In contrast, there was no difference between Republicans and Democrats: 56 percent of each approved. Of those who had heard about the Marshall Plan in July 1947, 67 percent of the college group, 55 percent of the high school group, and 49 percent of the grade school group approved. When asked in May 1949 whether the Senate should ratify the North Atlantic treaty, 80 percent of the college group, 73 percent of the high school group, and 58 percent of the grade school group supported ratification.[9]

Less important to the public generally than policy toward Russia and Western Europe was American policy toward Palestine and China. In May 1946, for example, only 50 percent had heard or read about the issue of Jewish migration into Palestine. When Gallup asked in December 1947, "If war breaks out between the Arabs and the Jews in Palestine, which side would you sympathize with?", a plurality of 38 percent said, "Neither," 26 percent had no opinion, 24 percent said, "Jews," and 12 percent said, "Arabs." Public opinion polls also showed strong support for keeping American troops out of the area and letting the United Nations try to resolve the conflict.[10]

Although the general public paid little attention to events in the Middle East and tended toward neutrality, the attentive public and opinion-makers were largely favorable toward the creation of a Jewish state in Palestine. Horrified by the extermination of millions of Jews by Nazi Germay and influenced by the work of pro-Zionist organizations like the American Zionist Emergency Council and the American Jewish Conference, many Congressmen, editors, and Protestant leaders strongly supported Zionist goals such as the large-scale migration of Jews to Palestine and the creation of a Jewish nation. Compared with the vigor and determination of the pro-Zionist organizations, anti-Zionist groups like the American Council for Judaism and the largely non-Jewish Committee for Justice and Peace in the Holy Land were weak and ineffective.[11]

The unfolding of American policy toward Palestine is a classic example of domestic influences upon foreign policy. Top officials in the State and Defense departments believed that the United States soon would need large quantities of Arab oil, and hence should not antagonize Arab leaders by supporting Zionist goals. Others within the government and elsewhere, however, strongly supported a Jewish homeland. As John Snetsinger has shown, Truman had no strong opinions on this issue and vacillated from 1945 to 1948 between measures supporting and opposing the Zionists. Vigorous Jewish lobbying, including the writing of hundreds of thousands of pro-Zionist letters and postcards, and especially the need to capture the Jewish vote in key northern states in the 1948 election, finally tipped Truman's policy toward a strongly pro-Israeli position by mid-1948. In January 1949 the administration granted the Israelis a $100 million loan and extended full diplomatic recognition to Israel.[12]

More Americans knew about the civil war in China than about events in Palestine, but the struggle between the Nationalists and the Communists never was viewed as the most important problem facing the nation by more than 2 percent of Gallup's respondents. Despite the efforts of lobbyists for Nationalist China and conservative newspapers and periodicals to build support for Chiang Kai-shek, many Americans had concluded by the late 1940s that the Nationalists were corrupt and deserved to lose if they could not rally the Chinese people against the Communists. As late as April 1948 a majority supported sending the Nationalists additional military supplies and financial aid; but by November of that year, as Nationalist losses mounted, a majority of those with opinions opposed sending $5 billion in additional aid. By May 1949 only 22 percent advocated further assistance to the Nationalists, and by August only 21 percent had a favorable opinion of Chiang Kai-shek. Despite this turnaround in public opinion, limited aid continued to be sent to the Nationalists.[13]

Most Americans also disliked the victorious Communists: in November 1949, for example, a majority believed that they "take their orders from Moscow." After the Communists established the People's Republic of China on October 1, 1949, the public opposed recognizing the new government by a margin of two to one.[14]

During the Korean War, which lasted from June 1950 until July 1953, partisan differences became more important than education as a guide to public opinion. The generally bipartisan approach to foreign policy practiced by Republican leaders since Pearl Harbor was weakened by the declining importance of the eastern wing of the party after Dewey's defeat in 1948 and by right-wing bitterness stemming from the "loss" of China. In February 1950 Republican Senator Joseph R. McCarthy began making sensational charges about Communists in the State Department and other executive agencies. Because of Communist gains abroad and because of fairly convincing evidence that Alger Hiss and some other former officials had spied for Russia in the past, McCarthy's warnings about Communists in government seemed plausible to many Americans despite his persistent failure to substantiate most of his charges. When it became clear by early 1951 that the Korean War had become unpopular, Republican leaders like Senator Robert A. Taft denounced administration policy, established an issue for the 1952 election, and helped to shape the attitudes of rank-and-file Republicans.

For the first few months of the war, overwhelming majorities of both Republicans and Democrats supported Truman's decision to send American troops to fight in Korea. A plurality of Gallup's respondents in September 1950 also believed that the war would be over within six months. The United States would have stopped aggression and, as General MacArthur predicted, the boys would be home by Christmas.[15]

But when the mainland Chinese entered the war in force in late November, the situation changed dramatically and support for the war plummeted. According to National Opinion Research Center polls, Republican support for the war dropped from 81 percent in September to 42 percent in December and Democratic support dropped from 84 percent to 62 percent. Gallup reported similar declines in support, with Republican support dropping from 64 percent in August to 32 percent in December. The percentage of those who approved Truman's performance as President declined from 43 percent in August 1950 to 26 percent (including only 13 percent of Republicans) in February 1951; the percentage who disapproved grew from 32 to 57 (including 75 percent of Republicans). For two full years—from January 1951 until Eisenhower became President in January 1953—the nation had both an unpopular war and a highly unpopular President.[16]

Most Americans—notably Republicans and the less well educated—consistently wanted an end to American involvement in the war. The majority of Americans in 1951 and 1952 considered entering the war a mistake, wanted to pull American troops out of Korea as rapidly as possible, and supported numerous proposals to achieve a negotiated peace. Only among the college-educated were there consistent majorities who believed that American involvement in the war had not been a mistake. In only one of the eight Gallup polls on the question between December 1950 and December 1952 did as many as 50 percent of Democrats answer that the war had not been a mistake, and in only two did as many as 40 percent of Republicans do so.[17]

Although most Americans probably did not want the United States to be defeated in Korea, proposals for a compromise peace were popular. The majority supported withdrawal of American troops if the Chinese agreed to withdraw their troops, greater efforts to start peace talks, a truce at the 38th parallel, and other plans to end the war. Partially because MacArthur promised a quick end to the war if mainland China was attacked, and partially because Truman was so unpopular, 66 percent disapproved Truman's firing of Mac-Arthur in April 1951.[18]

Why did the Korean War become unpopular among the mass public? There were many reasons, including frustration with a limited war in which the United States was fighting but the real enemy, Russia, was not. The war brought higher taxes, inflation, growing casualty lists, and a frustrating stalemate. It was being fought in a country most Americans knew virtually nothing about: only 3 percent, for example, knew the approximate size of South Korea's population in June 1951. Most Americans knew much more about the nations of Western Europe, and they repeatedly told public opinion interviewers in 1951 and 1952 that they considered it much more important to defend Western Europe against Communism than to defend Asia. What they wanted by the fall of 1952 was an anti-Communist President who would restore peace.[19]

Perhaps the most significant result of the American involvement in Korea was a substantial hardening of attitudes toward Russia and mainland China. The percentage believing that Russia was trying to become "the ruling power of the world" grew from 70 in January 1950 to 81 in November. Attitudes also hardened significantly against Communist China, which entered the war on the side of North Korea late in 1950, and in favor of the Nationalist government on

Taiwan, which by January 1951 the public as a whole considered a proper recipient of American military aid.[20]

Most Americans in the early 1950s also supported an enlarged military establishment even after the war ended, rearmament of Germany and Japan, and other measures reflecting a more hard-line, defense-oriented approach to the Cold War. Partly because of the hardening of attitudes which occurred during the Korean War, most Americans remained committed for at least another decade to the Cold War perspective on world affairs.[21]

Before describing trends in mass opinion from Eisenhower's election in the fall of 1952 through the Cuban missile crisis in the fall of 1962, it would seem appropriate to consider the views of the foreign policy activists—those who took public positions and sought to influence policy at mid-century. The dominant view from the late 1940s through the early 1960s had such powerful influence even on its critics that it may be called the Cold War consensus. But the views of the conservative, nationalist critics and the liberal, internationalist critics also were important in setting the parameters of the ongoing debate on American foreign policy.

The assumption shared by virtually all foreign policy activists in the post-World War II period was that the United States, the world's preeminent nation, had to take an active role in maintaining world order. Differences in approach to foreign policy among those holding this common assumption can be understood best in terms of what political scientists have called the unilateralist-multilateralist continuum. The nationalists on the unilateralist end of the continuum distrusted such policies as support for the United Nations and economic aid to developing nations. The internationalists at the multilateralist extreme believed that the only long-term hope for peace lay in transforming the United Nations into an effective world government. Those who adhered to the basic Cold War consensus were near the middle of the continuum. They supported forming alliances, working through the United Nations, and giving foreign aid—but only if these multilateralist policies clearly were promoting the American national interest.

One significant feature of the Cold War consensus was the reversal of alliances after 1945. All the former enemies—Germany, Japan, and Italy—became respected allies by 1950. Britain remained an ally, though perhaps not as important in American strategic thinking as Germany and Japan, but Russia and mainland China were both viewed as mortal enemies within a few years after the end of the war.

Because these erstwhile allies were believed to be committed to the spread of Communism and eventual world domination, the United States had to assume leadership of the "Free World" in order to "contain" the Communists. Particularly after the Communists won the Chinese civil war, those who adhered to the Cold War consensus believed that the United States must do everything in its power to prevent the spread of Communism in Asia, the Middle East, Africa, and Latin America, as well as in Europe. The formation of alliances on the perimeter of the Communist bloc, generous military and economic aid to allies, vigorous measures to maintain a favorable climate for American investment abroad, and covert operations to prevent Communist and other anti-American leaders from coming to power—all were fully acceptable to the editors, labor leaders, businessmen, educators, and others who strongly supported the foreign policies of the Truman, Eisenhower, and Kennedy administrations.

Although most adherents of the Cold War consensus believed that war with the Communist bloc was neither desirable nor inevitable, proposals to improve relations with Russia and China were viewed with skepticism or hostility. The Communists were inherently untrustworthy: conciliatory gestures on their part were at best tactical maneuvers, at worst camouflages to hide preparations for war. The United States and its allies must build up their defenses and remain militarily superior to the Communist bloc. Efforts by the Russians to improve their military technology tended to be viewed as attempts to achieve a first-strike nuclear capability. So rapid appeared to be the advance of military technology that newspaper columnists and politicians of the party out of power, briefed privately by proponents of new weapons systems, always could warn that Russia might be dangerously ahead within three to five years.

Belief in an evil and monolithic enemy did contribute to public support for many policies involving the expenditure of taxpayers' money which might not have been approved in more normal times. The threat of Communism was used as partial justification for the Marshall Plan, Point Four, and succeeding programs of economic aid to developing nations, tariff reduction and removal of other barriers to trade, and even private giving in the form of CARE packages and drives to raise money for nations ravaged by war or natural disasters. By the late 1950s the federal government not only had its own extensive program of foreign aid but it also contributed food, and paid shipping costs, for distribution abroad by private organizations such as the American Friends Service Committee.

The Cold War consensus on economic and military leadership of the non-Communist world was fostered by governmental publicity, generally supportive mass media, and cooperation from universities, economic and religious organizations, and such important organizations in the dissemination of information about foreign affairs as the Council on Foreign Relations and the Foreign Policy Association. Ironically, the Cold War consensus also was supported indirectly by Senator McCarthy and other opponents on the Right, who contributed substantially to the creation of an atmosphere in which dissent in the direction of support for recognition of Communist China, for example, generally was considered beyond the limits of responsible debate.

The Committee to Defend America by Aiding Anti-Communist China, the Committee of One Million Against the Admission of Communist China to the United Nations, and the other organizations and lobbyists which made up the "China lobby" in the Cold War years helped to build support for Chiang Kai-shek's government on Taiwan and opposition to any moves to improve relations with mainland China. Support for Chiang Kai-shek was strong among conservatives generally and in veterans' groups, which grew in membership and influence with the addition of millions of new members after World War II and the Korean War.[22]

The nationalistic, unilateralist challenge to the Cold War consensus centered on whether the West would have to be satisfied with the largely defensive policy of containing Communism, or whether at least some victories might be achieved in the struggle with the Communist world. If Communism was as evil and dictatorial as most Americans agreed that it was, then how could the majority of people in Russia and China—much less Eastern Europe—support it? Of what value was the West's preponderance of military power if Western leaders were afraid to use it? And why adopt a no-win policy in which Communists were permitted to seize power in countries like China and Cuba but non-Communists never were encouraged to seize power in Communist nations?

The view that containment was insufficient and that nations dominated by Russia could be "liberated" was especially appealing to Americans of East European descent. Determined to achieve victory after twenty years as the opposition party, the Republicans in 1952 denounced containment and vowed to work vigorously for self-determination in Eastern Europe. "The American conscience can never know peace until these people are restored again to being masters of their own fate," Eisenhower declared in a speech in New York City on August 25. Two days later, John Foster Dulles announced Eisenhower's support for liberation in Buffalo, a major center of Polish-Americans. Soon after Eisenhower's inauguration, however, it became clear that the new administration did not

1956: Despite Hungarian-American rallies and nationwide emotion, President Eisenhower forbore to challenge Soviet tanks in Budapest.

intend to use force to drive the Russians out of Eastern Europe. Any remaining hopes for liberation were quashed when the United States failed to support the Hungarian uprising in 1956.[23]

A virulently nationalistic, anti-Communist foreign policy was espoused in the 1950s and 1960s by such right-wing groups as the John Birch Society and the Liberty Lobby, and by such fundamentalist religious groups as Carl McIntire's Twentieth Century Reformation House and Billy James Hargis's Christian Crusade. Ultraconservative groups frequently bought air time on radio and television to advocate their viewpoint and to plead for contributions.

More respectable but equally anti-Communist were the views of James Burnham, whose regular column in the conservative magazine *National Review* was entitled "The Third World War." The war was in progress around the world, the Communists were winning, and they would continue to win until the West mounted a bold counteroffensive. "A tolerable peace . . . ," Senator Barry Goldwater wrote in his best-selling *Conscience of a Conservative* (1960), "must *follow* victory over Communism." [24]

What united more cautious nationalists like Senator Robert Taft and more belligerent ones like Burnham and Goldwater was belief in a unilateralist foreign policy. The United Nations frequently did more harm than good, and alliances were expensive and cumbersome. When the United States needed to move quickly and forcefully against a Communist threat, consulting with allies would be counterproductive. Instead of making the nation stronger, alliances such as the Organization of American States often made the United States weaker in dealing with countries like Cuba. The only guarantees of security in a threatening world were unimpeachable military strength and the willingness to use it.

Many foreign policy activists at the other end of the continuum disagreed totally with the nationalist approach. Members of such organizations as the United World Federalists believed that the nation-state system always had resulted in war, that atomic weapons had made war unthinkable, and that, therefore, some form of effective world government had to be established if the human race was to survive. As Grenville Clark and Louis B. Sohn wrote in *World Peace Through World Law* (1958), "If the world really wants peace, it must accept world institutions adequate to achieve complete disarmament and to enforce world law within the limited field of war prevention." Founded in 1947, United World Federalists had 40,000 members in local chapters throughout the country by 1951. Although the organization declined after the early 1950s, Norman Cousins, the liberal editor of *Saturday Review,* continued to publicize world federalist objectives, and many internationalist organizations such as the Council for a Liveable World and the Institute for World Order, active during the 1960s and 1970s, carried on its ideals by concentrating on the realization of limited portions of the federalist program.[25]

While the federalists worked for the long-range goal of a world government based on the model of the American constitution, other multilateralists and peace advocates sought more immediate accomplishments. The American Association for the United Nations, whose most famous organizer was Eleanor Roosevelt, established chapters across the country and built support for strengthening the United Nations. In the late 1950s the AAUN challenged the Cold War consensus and infuriated leaders of the "China Lobby" by calling for a re-evaluation of American policy toward mainland China. The Federation of American Scientists, founded in 1946, persistently warned of the dangers of nuclear testing in its respected magazine, *Bulletin of the Atomic Scientists,* and through lobbying and publicity.[26]

By the late 1950s the Federation of American Scientists, the National Committee for a Sane Nuclear Policy (SANE), and other peace and church groups were calling for the suspension of nuclear testing by both the United States and Russia as a first step toward halting the arms race. A more radical group loosely associated with SANE, the Committee for Nonviolent Action, demonstrated against nuclear testing in the late 1950s by sailing two small boats toward the American testing area in the Pacific and by staging sit-ins at missile bases in Wyoming and Nebraska.

In the wake of growing public concern about nuclear fallout and the continuation of the arms race, President Eisenhower in August 1958 announced a one-year moratorium on testing. Two months later representatives of the United States, Britain, and Russia began test-ban negotiations in Geneva. Despite differences in outlook, advances followed by setbacks, and frequent recesses, the negotiations developed momentum and led ultimately to the Test Ban Treaty of 1963, a breakthrough in relations between Russia and the West.

The test-ban negotiations, Eisenhower's meetings with Russian leaders, and some other developments of the 1950s were steps away from Cold War confrontation. Despite its anti-Communist rhetoric, its military intervention in Lebanon, and its secret paramilitary operations in countries ranging from Guatemala to Vietnam, the Eisenhower administration pursued a course in foreign affairs that was partially compatible with a conviction growing in strength among liberals: peaceful coexistence with Russia was both possible and desirable.

During the Eisenhower and Kennedy years relations with the Soviet Union continued to dominate both official and public perceptions of American foreign policy. Other issues—notably Indochina, the Middle East, the Chinese offshore islands, Cuba, and the Congo—frequently made the headlines; but even these tended to be viewed largely as Cold War issues involving tests of strength between the United States and Russia rather than as localized problems. The general trend in American opinion during these years was toward the idea that the United States and Russia could resolve their differences peacefully. But these were also the years in which

1959: Khrushchev's American visit was a high point in the post-Stalin thaw, but a relieved public kept its fingers crossed.

—from *Straight Herblock*
(Simon & Schuster, 1964)

the word *crisis* became a favorite term to describe almost any East-West disagreement. And Americans generally assumed that any of these crises—Indochina, Suez, Lebanon, the Congo, Berlin, Cuba, and others—could evolve quickly into World War III.

One way to approach public thinking about world affairs during these years is to consider polls on the probability of war. During the 1950s majorities consistently believed that there would be another world war in their lifetime. From 1953 through 1955, and again in the early 1960s, majorities of those with opinions believed that there would be a world war within five years. By the late 1950s most Americans believed that hydrogen bombs would be dropped on major population centers in the United States if war broke out, and most also doubted their own chances of survival. A 1961 poll gives some indication of public anxiety: 22 percent said they were "very worried" and another 37 percent said they were "fairly worried" about the possibility of atomic war.[27]

A more positive approach to attitudes toward Russia is to consider the growing percentages of respondents who believed that the United States could "live peacefully" with Russia. In the fall of 1954 and the winter of 1955 the percentage stood at 23, but it grew to 35 by October 1955 in the wake of Eisenhower's summit conference with Russian and other Western leaders that summer. Gallup did not pose the question again for several years, but after Soviet Premier Nikita Khrushchev's visit to the United States in the late summer of 1959 the percentage believing it possible to "reach a peaceful settlement of differences between Russia and the West" had risen to 66. When basically the same question was asked in December 1960 and twice during 1962, majorities continued to believed that peaceful coexistence with Russia was possible.[28]

During the 1950s the public consistently supported summit meetings between Russian and American leaders to ease world tensions. Beginning with the "thaw" of 1955, which included not only the summit meeting but also cultural exchanges between the two superpowers, the public regularly supported agricultural, tourist, educational, athletic, and other exchange programs. Support for trade with Russia grew from 40 percent of the public in August 1953 to 55 percent in June 1955. Support for Russian-American trade declined somewhat before reaching 55 percent again in February 1959.[29]

During the late 1940s the college-educated had provided the greatest support for containment policies such as the Truman Doctrine and the Marshall Plan; during the 1950s the college-educated consistently gave the most support to proposals to ease East-West tensions. In the June 1955 poll on trade with Russia, for example, 70 percent of the college-educated, as opposed to 53 percent of the high school group and 50 percent of the grade school group, supported the establishment of commercial ties with Russia. In October 1955, the percentage believing peaceful coexistence was possible ranged from 51 percent of the college group to 23 percent of the grade school group. The college-educated—those most likely to be involved in foreign policy issues and to have influential positions in their own communities—initiated during the 1950s the long process of moderating hostile public attitudes toward Russia.[30]

During the late 1950s and early 1960s there was considerable concern among the attentive public that the United States was losing the Cold War. The launching of Sputnik I in October 1957 surprised many who had considered America's technology inherently superior to Russia's. It also raised the question of whether the United States faced a "missile gap" in which the American capacity to retaliate could be largely destroyed by a surprise attack. Joseph Alsop, a widely read newspaper columnist, predicted in 1958 that Russia would have one hundred intercontinental ballistic missiles to zero for the United States in 1959, and that by 1963 Russia would have two thousand to only one hundred thirty for the United States. The "missile gap" was only one part of a more general argument, advanced by Democratic Senators John F. Kennedy and Henry M. Jackson among others, that the United States needed to increase defense expenditures substantially to meet the Communist threat.[31]

Even if they had been able to judge the relative military value of all the new bombs and missiles, the people as a whole still would not have been sure whether the United States was falling behind Russia, as the Democratic Senators charged, or whether American defenses were more than adequate, as Eisenhower and other administration officials insisted. The public also had no reliable way to evaluate whether, as many journalists and academics contended, the Russians were engaged in a systematic effort to spread Communism to the developing nations. With the possible exception of his misinterpreted "we will bury you" remark, nothing Khrushchev ever said more influenced American policy-makers, and nothing was more widely quoted in the mass media, than his comment in a speech in January 1961 that Russia supported "wars of national liberation." If civil war erupted anywhere in the Free

World, many Americans reasoned, Russia and mainland China had to be encouraging the insurgents.

During the late 1950s and early 1960s East-West conflict in Europe centered on West Berlin, which Khrushchev viewed as a "bone in the throat" of the Soviet bloc and which officials in Washington considered the critical test of America's determination to defend the Free World. Until they built a wall in August 1961 to seal off their sector of Berlin, the Russians and East Germans were concerned about the flight of large numbers of young, skilled East Germans to West Germany via West Berlin; they also wanted the Western powers to grant some form of recognition to the East German government. But speeches by American leaders and coverage of the issue in the media almost invariably suggested that the only Russian objective was to force the United States and its allies to abandon West Berlin to the Communists. At times, as in 1961 when Khrushchev threatened to sign a separate peace treaty with East Germany and Kennedy responded by increasing military expenditures and calling up the reserves, both sides were bellicose; at other times, seemingly interminable negotiations took place and Berlin dropped out of the headlines. When the news reporting did cover Berlin, it emphasized conflicts between Russian and American troops and daring escapes by East Germans; as usual, the media provided little insight into the underlying issues in the dispute.

The vast majority of Americans supported their government's determination to stand firm on Berlin, which since the late 1940s had been a major symbol of the Cold War. In March 1959, 78 percent of Americans were familiar with the Berlin conflict; by August 1961, 90 percent—an unusually high percentage for a foreign policy issue—were aware of the conflict. More than 80 percent in 1959 and again in 1961 supported keeping American forces in Berlin even at the risk of war, and large majorities also were willing to fight if the access routes to Berlin were closed. Although the Cold War atmosphere and the nature of media coverage impeded full understanding of the issues involved, the American people backed the Eisenhower and Kennedy administrations' handling of relations with Russia on Berlin.[32]

Despite persistent tensions between the United States and Russia in regard to Berlin, many attentive Americans viewed the balance of power in Europe as relatively stable and considered the developing nations as the primary battlegrounds of the Cold War. Because Communism thrived on hunger and deprivation, could the United States channel enough foreign aid to these societies before the Communists won? How could the United States induce the ruling classes to make the reforms necessary to win popular support? What were the best ways to fight the guerrillas?

Social scientists and public officials pondered these questions, but both they and the general public were limited by lack of knowledge of the particular societies for which general answers were being formulated. Where were Laos and British Guiana, and which nations bordered on the Congo? Many policy-makers and columnists in the late 1950s and early 1960s might have been able to answer these questions, but they definitely knew little about the history and balance of political and cultural forces within most of the developing nations with which the United States felt compelled to become involved.

During the Eisenhower and Kennedy years the public generally wanted to contain Communism, but it also wanted to keep out of war. When asked by pollsters what the government should do about particular trouble spots in the developing world, the public almost invariably approved sending military and other forms of aid, but opposed sending American troops. When asked in May 1953 whether to send war materials to assist the French in Indochina, 56 percent said, "Yes"; when asked whether to send American soldiers to take part in the fighting, only 12 percent said, "Yes" and 78 percent said, "No." When asked in May 1954 what the United

States "would gain by getting into a fighting war in Indochina," by far the largest response was "nothing." [33]

The public in November 1953 opposed entering the fighting if South Korea attacked North Korea, but it would send war materials to the South Koreans. In September 1956 a majority opposed entering the fighting if England and France attacked Egypt. In May 1961 a plurality of 44 percent were willing to give military supplies to anti-Castro forces, but 65 percent opposed the use of American troops to aid in overthrowing Castro. In September 1962, on the eve of the Cuban missile crisis, a substantial majority still opposed an American invasion of Cuba.[34]

This is not to suggest that the public during the Cold War years was as noninterventionist as it was in the 1930s, for then the majority had opposed military aid. Moreover, if Eisenhower or Kennedy had decided to commit troops in any of these situations, there is every reason to believe that an overwhelming majority would have supported the President for at least the first few months of war. Both Eisenhower and Kennedy were highly popular even among the rank-and-file members of the opposing party, and both were supported in moments of embarrassment as well as of triumph. Despite the fact that the Eisenhower administration was caught lying during the U-2 incident in May 1960, 58 percent said that the administration handled the situation well. Similarly, the percentage approving Kennedy's performance as President rose immediately after the ill-fated Bay of Pigs invasion of Cuba in April 1961. What Arthur M. Schlesinger, Jr., has called the "imperial presidency" could count on broad popular support for most foreign policy decisions.[35]

An illustration of a popular President's power to influence public opinion was Kennedy's decision in early March 1962 to resume nuclear testing in the atmosphere. Despite the fact that Russia's resumption of testing in September 1961 was unpopular and well-publicized, only 44 percent of Gallup's re-

October 1962: TV appeals to the nation from the Oval Office, like President Kennedy's during the Cuban missile crisis, are now a familiar leadership device.

United Press International

spondents in November 1961 supported American atmospheric tests, while 45 percent opposed them. Two months later, after there had been considerable pressure from some Congressmen and others to resume testing, the favorable percentage had risen only two points to 46, and the percentage opposed had dropped two points to 43. After Kennedy explained his reasons for ordering the resumption on nationwide television, 66 percent approved and only 25 percent opposed atmospheric testing.[36]

An even more dramatic illustration of Presidential leadership during the Cold War occurred the following autumn. On October 22, 1962, Kennedy went on television to demand that the Soviet Union remove its missiles from Cuba, to announce an American blockade of Cuba that would prevent the arrival of additional missiles, and to mobilize American public opinion behind a policy that clearly risked nuclear war. Informal polls taken during the next few days showed that an anxious public overwhelmingly supported the administration in its showdown with Russia. Soviet leaders had two basic choices: back down and accept a humiliating defeat, or go to war with the United States. There was a feeling of relief—and, for some, of gratitude—when Khrushchev agreed to remove the missiles.

5

RECOGNIZING LIMITS,
1963–1978

Until a few years ago I was an anti-communist liberal who believed in the necessity of "maintaining our commitments against the forces of communism." Troublesome questions arose in my mind but these were usually vanquished by my deeply conditioned reactions to fearful images of the "cold-war struggle," and "communist aggression." Vietnam was for me, as for many other Americans, a crucible for my anti-communist beliefs. I began reading about the Vietnam war still convinced that "aggression" had to be stopped. The more I studied the problem, the more I found myself questioning not only our involvement in that conflict but also the whole train of attitudes and events that brought us to it. Eventually I found I could no longer consider myself an adherent of the anti-communism preached and practiced by American liberals and conservatives.

—MICHAEL PARENTI (1969) [1]

FOR MANY AMERICANS the Vietnam War was the major catalyst for a general re-evaluation of the assumptions upon which the Cold War consensus had been built, but it definitely was not the only factor contributing to changing attitudes toward American foreign policy. Improved relations with Russia in the aftermath of the Cuban missile crisis, the open split between Russia and mainland China, changes in the Western alliance, the emergence of a new generation of Americans who remembered neither Munich nor the Czechoslovakian coup—these and other developments of the 1960s contributed to the drift away from the dominant Cold War approach. When in 1972 President Nixon visited mainland China and Russia and national security adviser Henry Kissinger declared repeatedly the benefits of détente, the Cold War as practiced for a generation clearly was not its old self.

More than in any of the three previous shifts in American foreign policy, the shift in the dominant assumptions which occurred between the mid-1960s and 1972 involved interaction between domestic concerns and international developments. Even before the buildup of American troops in Vietnam in 1965, liberals had begun to stress the need to "reorder national priorities"—to devote less thought and resources to international relations, the space race, and defense, and to concentrate more on helping minorities, eradicating poverty, and improving education and health care. "While the cold war and our enormously costly national security programs pre-empt so much of our time and attention and national wealth," Senator J. William Fulbright wrote in *Old Myths and New Realities* (1964), "the most important resources of our country—its human resources—are being extravagantly wasted and neglected." Such sentiments appeared in the press as early as 1963, but they gained broad support only when the Vietnam War became costly and urban riots and radical dissent demonstrated deep divisions within American society. When by the late 1960s the stock market tended to rally in the wake of peace rumors, it was clear that even those who were not committed liberals believed that the United States needed to curtail its international commitments and concentrate on dealing with pressing domestic problems.[2]

Just as it was easier in the 1920s to reject American membership in the League of Nations than to fashion a coherent, broadly supported foreign policy, so in recent years it has been easier to discredit Cold War assumptions than to define new guiding principles for American policy. Since the return of the last combat troops from Vietnam in 1973, the public as a whole has been more interested in domestic than in foreign policy issues. Without the focus provided by anti-Communism and Asian wars, the attentive public has developed a multitude of foreign policy interests ranging from the sharing of world resources to concern about America's defense posture. During the past decade Americans have come to realize that their nation does not possess unlimited economic or military power, but most have not felt compelled to think through the implications of this fact. If the past provides a clue to the future, the eventual focusing of public attitudes will result more from events abroad and domestic developments which affect Americans directly than from advocacy of one foreign policy program or another.

The most important outgrowth of the Cuban missile crisis was improved Soviet-American relations. In 1963 alone, the United States and Russia established a "hot line" communications system between Washington and Moscow, signed a treaty to end nuclear testing in the atmosphere, and substantially increased the level of bilateral trade. Even before these steps were taken, however, public opinion polls, editorials, speeches, letters to the editor, and other indicators of attitudes suggested that the American people, sobered by the close brush with nuclear war, wanted to improve relations with Russia. In December 1962, 63 percent of Gallup's respondents believed that the United States and Russia would be able to settle their differences peacefully. Solid majorities during 1963 approved Senate ratification of the test ban treaty, favored the sale of surplus wheat to Russia, and believed that direct airline passenger service should be established between the two nations. When Louis Harris asked in March 1965 whether Russia was more or less favorable toward peace than a few years before, 44 percent said "more for peace" and only 2 percent said "less for peace." [3]

A major reason for more favorable attitudes toward Russia was the feeling in the aftermath of the missile crisis that the United States finally had won a major victory in the Cold War and had proved that it was the preeminent power. When asked in December 1962 whether America's power in the world would increase or decrease in 1963, 82 percent said it would increase and only 5 percent said it would decrease. The percentage believing that Russian power would increase in 1963 was 35, whereas the percentage believing it would decrease was 45. As Lloyd A. Free and Hadley Cantril discovered in an in-depth poll in the fall of 1964, many Americans strongly believed that the United States, as one respondent put it, must "remain at the top—the very best and looked-up-to nation in the world." [4]

The generally more favorable attitudes toward Russia, which for President Lyndon Johnson included a desire to "build bridges across the gulf which has divided us from Eastern Europe," were not shared by everyone. The AFL-CIO, strongly anti-Communist and fearful of imports from Eastern Europe, was opposed to increased trade, as were such groups as the American Legion and the militantly conservative Young Americans for Freedom. Continuing Cold War attitudes were reflected in a 1964 publication of the American Bar Association entitled *Peaceful Coexistence: A Communist Blueprint for Victory* and in the nomination of Senator Barry Goldwater as the Republican candidate for President. For many, however, such terms as "Communist world" or "the Communists" had replaced "Russia" or "the Soviet Union" as symbols of evil. [5]

In addition to improving Soviet-American relations, the Cuban missile crisis reduced the intensity of American hatred of Fidel Castro. Americans in 1961 and 1962 generally had viewed Castro as an unpopular dictator, a puppet of Russian leaders, and an affront to the United States. Republican politicians and right-wing organizations repeatedly had insisted that the Kennedy administration "do something" about Castro, the clear implication being that American honor would not be restored until Castro was overthrown. But if Castro could not be toppled without taking more drastic measures than most Americans were prepared to advocate, the aware ness that the missiles were being removed despite Castro's strong protests mollified many Americans.

Even before Kennedy's assassination in November 1963, it had become clear to anyone at all interested in international relations that both the Communist bloc and the Western alliance were in disarray. The thinly disguised animosity between Russia and China burst into public view in 1962 and 1963 as the two nations traded bitter accusations. After French President Charles de Gaulle blocked British membership in the Common Market in January 1963, a plurality of 35 percent of Gallup's respondents said that France no longer was a reliable ally. By June 1966, when de Gaulle's criticisms of American leadership of NATO were well-known, 56 percent held this view, while only 16 percent believed that France was reliable.[6]

By the mid-1960s, in short, few could doubt that the largely bipolar world of the 1950s was giving way to a more polycentric distribution of power. But as American policy toward the Dominican Republic, mainland China, and Vietnam demonstrated, officials in the Johnson administration were more comfortable proceeding with policies based on Cold War assumptions than attempting to make policies based on new, untested assumptions.

Continuing preoccupation with Communism, together with the patronizing Uncle-Sam-knows-best attitude which had characterized much of American opinion of Latin America for many decades, was demonstrated in 1965 when President Johnson, fearful of a possible Communist takeover, dispatched troops to the Dominican Republic. Gallup found that 76 percent supported American military intervention, and Harris reported that overwhelming majorities favored forcing the Dominicans to form a coalition government meeting American specifications and keeping the troops there until a stable government was established. Although a majority of those with opinions in November 1965 acknowledged that American intervention had harmed relations with other Latin American nations, nearly three-fourths of those with opinions believed that the United States had done the "right thing" in sending troops.[7]

American attitudes toward mainland China during the 1960s reflected the tension between the continuing influence of Cold War assumptions and increasing pressure for a reevaluation of American policy. Differences in opinion surfaced within the government as Fulbright and other members of the increasingly independent Senate Foreign Relations Committee challenged the continuing policy of isolating mainland China, while orthodox Cold Warriors like Secretary of State Dean Rusk insisted on maintaining the policy he had helped to establish during the Truman years. To the Johnson administration, containment of mainland China was a primary goal of American policy in Vietnam; to the administration's critics, efforts to isolate mainland China were a basic source of America's difficulties in Asia.

The debate during the mid-1960s on American policy toward China also involved a large portion of the attentive public. Although less influential than during the 1950s, the Committee of One Million continued to pressure Congressmen to oppose any change in America's China policy. The Committee's promise of retribution at the polls for anyone wavering in his support of Chiang Kai-shek became less and less credible as the 1960s progressed. Conservative periodicals like the *Reader's Digest* continued to feature articles warning of the dangers of having any dealings with the Communist Chinese, but others, such as the *Saturday Evening Post*, began to adopt a more even-handed approach. There were more television documentaries and magazine articles on conditions in mainland China, more symposia sponsored by universities and civic groups, and more pressures for changes in policy from liberal organizations like Americans for Democratic Action and the Friends Committee on National Legislation. Although the Peking government officially remained hostile to the United States throughout the 1960s, pressures for a change in American policy developed a strong momentum.[8]

What did the general public think of mainland China in the 1960s? The most common feeling probably was increasing concern. Mainland China had a huge population, it was developing atomic weapons, and its government was anti-American. When Gallup asked in March 1963, "Looking ahead to 1970, which country do you think will be the greater threat to world peace—Russia or Communist China?", 49 percent said Russia and 32 percent said China. A year later, however, 59 percent answered China and 32 percent answered Russia to the same question; by February 1967, 71 percent answered China while only 20 percent answered Russia. This shift, especially the large change from early 1963 to early 1964, clearly reflected growing détente with Russia coupled with increasing fear of Chinese military power. "I think Russia will hold off, but I am worried about China," one respondent told Free and Cantril in the fall of 1964. "The Chinese place no value on life." [9]

Public opinion on China, as on so many other foreign policy issues, tended to divide mainly according to level of education. A poll by the Survey Research Center in mid-1964 found that 48 percent of those with college degrees favored "dealing with the Communist government as the government of most of China," whereas only 21 percent of the grade school group supported such a policy. When asked in December 1965 whether mainland China should be admitted to the United Nations, the overall response was 22 percent yes, 67 percent no, and 16 percent no opinion. But the percentages for the college group were 35, 61, and 4, whereas the percentages for the grade school group were 13, 68, and 19. By January 1969, 49 percent of the college group, compared with 31 percent of the high school group and 21 percent of the grade school group, favored U.N. membership for the mainland Chinese. As in the 1950s on changes in Soviet-American relations, the better educated led the way in the 1960s toward improved relations with mainland China.[10]

Although level of education was the best indicator of attitudes toward changing America's China policy, such factors as political affiliation, age, and sex also were fairly important. Those who were independent or moderately Democratic in political outlook were the most likely to favor improved relations with mainland China. Because support for Chiang Kai-shek long had been strongest among conservative Republican Congressmen, one would not expect most Republicans to favor improvement in relations with Peking. The Survey Research Center poll found that support for dealing with the Peking government declined with age; support dropped from 44 percent in the 34 and under age group, to 39 percent in the 35–44 age group, to 29 percent in the 45–54 age group, to 27 percent in the 55–64 age group, and to 18 percent among those aged 65 and over. Finally, 31 percent of men, but only 17 percent of women, responded that the United States should "deal with Chiang Kai-shek's government on Formosa as the government of all China, and have nothing to do with Communist China." [11]

Except at universities where New Left or conservative organizations were particularly active, most college students in the mid-1960s did not have fixed views on China. As one Oregon professor put it: "Students don't seem to have strong opinions but tend to think it foolish not to recognize China." Many older people and Republicans, in contrast, strongly opposed admitting mainland China to the United Nations, much less establishing diplomatic relations with this largely unknown but frightening nation.[12]

Despite the fact that more polls are available and more social scientists have attempted to analyze attitudes toward the Vietnam War than toward any other development in recent American history, analysis of public opinion on Vietnam remains quite difficult. Large segments of the public maintained contradictory goals: a strong desire for peace combined with unwillingness to accept an American defeat, for example, or a wish to support the President in wartime combined with distrust of his credibility. The war also became tied inextricably to domestic issues such as the values of college students and the claim by a vocal minority that the United States was a "sick" society for which the only appropriate treatment was revolution. The only safe generalization is that the longer this seemingly endless war lasted, the greater were public disaffection and support for terminating American involvement.

One of the questions pollsters asked most frequently during the Vietnam War was this: "In view of the developments since we entered the fighting in Vietnam, do you think the U.S. made a mistake sending troops to fight in Vietnam?" In August 1965, as the United States was rapidly increasing its involvement in the war, 61 percent said, "No" and 24 percent said, "Yes." For the next two years, between 48 and 59 percent continued to believe that the United States had not erred in entering the fighting in Vietnam. The Gallup poll in December 1967 was the final time that the respondents who answered "not a mistake" were more numerous than the respondents who answered "mistake," but only by a margin of 46 to 45. By March 1968, in the wake of the Tet offensive, the percentage answering "mistake" had grown to 49, while the percentage answering "not a mistake" had dropped to 41. By August 1968 only 35 percent believed that American involvement in Vietnam had not been a mistake, and by May

November 1967: As controversy deepened over Vietnam, President Johnson assumed a fighting stance in his televised news conference.

1971 the percentage had dropped even further to 28.[13]

Although no single question was asked throughout the war to ascertain the public's policy preferences, the evidence suggests that 1968 and 1969 were the key years for attitude change. From 1965 through 1967 the majority supported strong military action to achieve American objectives in Vietnam. As late as October 1967, a majority responded that the United States "should increase the strength of its attacks on North Vietnam." But after the Tet offensive in early 1968 appeared to have shattered hopes for a decisive military victory, the majority favored the more defensive strategy of preventing a Communist victory. By 1969 a desire to withdraw American troops from Vietnam had begun to predominate, and by early 1970 the majority supported withdrawal either immediately or within eighteen months regardless of whether South Vietnam survived as a nation.[14]

A frequent theme in discussion of the Vietnam War is that public opposition increased as casualties mounted during the Johnson years and decreased as casualties declined during the Nixon years. Although this view has some merit, it fails to account for continued strong public support for American objectives in Vietnam through the end of 1967 despite heavy casualties, and also for mounting opposition to remaining in Vietnam to achieve Nixon's objectives, despite shorter casualty lists.

More important than the number of casualties in increasing public dissatisfaction was the growing feeling that the war was unwinnable. Most Americans as early as 1965 and 1966 believed that the war would end in some kind of compromise; they repeatedly answered that the United States was "standing still" rather than "making progress" in the war; and they persistently doubted that the South Vietnamese could establish a stable government. The measures which they supported and which their leaders said would bring results—bombing North Vietnam, for example—did not appear to bring peace any closer. Both the generals in Vietnam and their civilian superiors in Washington lost credibility as the "light at the end of the tunnel" turned out to be an illusion.[15]

Describing the generally downward trend in support for the war is easier than drawing distinctions within the public in regard to attitudes toward the war. For some people, party affiliation was most important: Democrats were more likely to support Johnson's policy than were Republicans, and the reverse was true during the Nixon years. Others, having no consistent views on Vietnam or believing that the government knew best, were what John E. Mueller has called "followers": they tended to support the President regardless of whether he was calling for stepped-up bombing or a bombing halt. In general, women were more dovish than men, blacks were more dovish than whites, and Jews were more dovish than Protestants and Catholics.[16]

Although the usual demographic variables provide some insights into attitudes on Vietnam, the key difference appears to have been whether a person was liberal or conservative in his general approach to foreign policy. By the late 1960s most liberals no longer accepted Cold War rationales to justify American policy in Vietnam, whereas most conservatives still believed that the United States had the responsibility to contain Communism and, by keeping its commitments, to retain its credibility as leader of the Free World.

Attitudes toward the Vietnam War may be placed in the context of major approaches to American foreign policy in the period since World War II roughly as follows: foreign policy liberals who had been near the multilateralist end of the unilateralist-multilateralist continuum in the 1950s generally opposed American policy in Vietnam; foreign policy conservatives who had been at the other end of the continuum tended to support official policy; and adherents of the Cold War consensus on foreign policy near the center of the continuum—Clark Clifford and Hubert Humphrey are prominent examples—first supported and then opposed both American policy and the assumptions underlying it.

Divisions on Vietnam between liberals and conservatives were apparent in such institutions as labor unions, universities, and churches. More conservative unions like the Teamsters strongly supported the war, but more liberal ones like the United Auto Workers opposed it. College students from upper-middle-class liberal families, concentrated in the more prestigious colleges and universities, tended toward active opposition to the war, while students at colleges and universities with more modest reputations tended to support the war or at least not to demonstrate against it. A study of Protestant ministers conducted in 1968 found that 76 percent who described themselves as fundamentalist supported a greater military effort in order to win the war, while only 8 percent of liberals supported this position. Conversely, 42 percent of the liberals and 3 percent of the fundamentalists supported complete withdrawal.[17]

Most religious leaders, like others who had supported the Cold War consensus, probably shifted with the times. In 1967, for example, the delegates to the Southern Baptist Convention resolved to support the prosecution of the war until "an honorable and just peace could be achieved." A year later, in the aftermath of the Tet offensive, the convention "urged leaders on all sides of the Vietnam War to seek an immediate cease-fire, a termination of all hostile activities and no further buildup of military power." [18]

Divisions on Vietnam policy in Congress also were more pronounced between liberals and conservatives than between Republicans and Democrats. Liberal Democrats such as George McGovern and Allard Lowenstein became outspoken opponents of American policy in Vietnam, whereas conservative Democrats like John Stennis and James Eastland supported both Democratic and Republican Presidents on the war. Republican conservatives like Barry Goldwater and John Ashbrook joined conservative Democrats in supporting the war effort, while liberal Republicans like Mark Hatfield and Charles Percy criticized American involvement. Although more leaders of the generally more liberal Democratic Party came to oppose the war, organizers of both prowar and antiwar rallies were able to arrange to have prominent members of both parties address their gatherings.

Because it became controversial so quickly and lasted so long, the Vietnam War sparked more public involvement than any other foreign policy issue in American history. Not since the years leading up to American involvement in World War II had Americans been so concerned about their nation's foreign policy; never before had so many Americans participated in marches, rallies, teach-ins, draft-card burnings, and other events designed to affect the course of American foreign policy.

Although most of these events involved protesters against the war, it must not be forgotten that large numbers of Americans participated in prowar parades and other activities sponsored by the American Legion, Veterans of Foreign Wars, and other generally conservative groups. Like the Johnson and Nixon administrations, the prowar groups generally were on the defensive; their calls to "support our boys" often included no reasons why the public also should support the war. Displaying miniature American flag decals on car windows and clothing and placing "America: Love It or Leave It" stickers on bumpers symbolized the divisiveness of the war, as did the insertion of the swastika in place of the middle letter in Nixon's name in antiwar banners and such taunts by antiwar demonstrators as "Hey, hey, LBJ, how many kids did you kill today?"

Many of the organizations which opposed the Vietnam War had gained experience in challenging official policy during the campaign in the late 1950s and early 1960s to stop nuclear testing and slow the arms race. SANE, founded in 1957, and SDS, which held its first national convention in 1962, both questioned Cold War assumptions and participated in demonstrations and lobbying against nuclear testing. By the mid-1960s these and other organizations were well prepared to challenge official rationales for stepped-up American military involvement in Vietnam and to assist in organizing the many large-scale demonstrations which began soon after the escalation of the war in the spring of 1965.

Many of those who demonstrated against the war never formally joined any of the numerous antiwar organizations and splinter groups which attempted to coordinate the protest movement between 1965 and 1972. Many among the large numbers of young people in what was generally called the Movement were suspicious of organizations, but some types of organization clearly were required to coordinate antiwar activities. Persistent tensions between liberals in organizations like SANE and Clergy and Laity Concerned about Vietnam and radicals in organizations like SDS and the Progressive Labor Party prevented the achievement of unity among the anti-Vietnam activists. Although the radicals tended to be dedicated and energetic, many liberals feared that close association with Marxists and other radicals would permit conservatives to discredit the entire antiwar movement.

Because of fragmentation within the antiwar movement, umbrella organizations were formed to coordinate particular demonstrations. The National Mobilization Committee to End the War in Vietnam, for example, organized the large-scale march on the Pentagon in October 1967 which ended in a violent confrontation between demonstrators and military authorities. The largest series of demonstrations were organized in the fall of 1969 by the generally liberal Vietnam Moratorium Committee and the generally radical New Mobilization Committee. On October 15, 1969, more than one million people demonstrated against the war in cities across the country; a month later as many as half a million Americans participated in a mammoth, sometimes violent antiwar rally and a dignified "March Against Death" in Washington. Many Congressmen and others who watched the violent highlights on the evening news were shocked by the apparent anti-Americanism of a small minority of the demonstrators, who

1969: President Nixon's policy of disengagement from Vietnam was not enough to stop demonstrations against an unpopular war.

The New York Times

committed such acts as tearing down the flags at the Justice Department. Determined not to give the appearance of being affected by the largest demonstration ever held in Washington, President Nixon announced that he had spent the afternoon watching a football game.[19]

Because the most prominent antiwar activists were liberals or radicals on domestic issues as well as on Vietnam, the Nixon administration sought to mobilize support for continued involvement in Vietnam by identifying with the "silent majority" of ordinary Americans who distrusted demonstrators and "hippies." In a series of well-publicized speeches in 1969 and 1970, Vice-President Spiro Agnew led the attack against the "rotten apples" and "nattering nabobs of negativism" who were criticizing Nixon's policy of gradually turning the fighting over to the South Vietnamese. The stereotype of the antiwar activist—young, long-haired, pampered, and unpatriotic—made a perfect target for Agnew's attacks.[20]

Because demonstrations against the war sometimes were followed by increased support in the polls for official policy, public opinion analysts frequently argued that the more militant activists harmed their own cause. Undoubtedly this argument has some validity. But the demonstrators and activists like Philip and Daniel Berrigan and Benjamin Spock, by drawing media coverage to antiwar activities and by insisting that American involvement in Vietnam was a moral issue, helped to make the generally inattentive mass public aware that the war threatened to tear American society apart. By taking forward positions, the activists also helped to make it possible for others to take moderate but increasingly antiwar positions.

Perhaps the most profound result of the Vietnam War and the controversy over it that raged at home was the effect it had on American thinking about foreign affairs. The public in the late 1960s and early 1970s accelerated its shift away from support for the full range of Cold War policies. There was growing reluctance to become involved in military actions abroad, there was growing skepticism about governmental policy, and there was less support for military spending, foreign aid, and the United Nations. "Although the feeling has grown that the nation should concentrate more on domestic than on international problems, it would be an oversimplification to label this mood 'isolationism,' " Albert H. Cantril and Charles W. Roll, Jr. observed in 1971. "Rather, the public is critical and discriminating in assessing foreign commitments; its mood appears to range between noninterventionism and selective interventionism." [21]

Both continued internationalism and a desire to lessen military commitments were demonstrated in Gallup polls conducted in January 1969. When asked whether the United States should "keep independent in world affairs" or "work closely with other nations," 72 percent chose the latter. But 62 percent also said that the United States should not send troops if a situation like Vietnam were to develop elsewhere.[22]

War weariness also was apparent in a 1972 poll which found that a bare majority of 52 percent supported military defense of Western Europe against a Soviet attack, and only 43 percent supported defending Japan if that nation was attacked by Russia or mainland China. Those who agreed that "we shouldn't think so much in *international* terms but concentrate more on our own *national* problems and building up our strength and prosperity here at home" grew from 55 percent in 1964 to 60 percent in 1968 to 73 percent in 1972.[23]

Foreign aid, never one of the more popular programs even at the height of the Cold War, lost public support during the Vietnam period. The percentage which generally supported foreign aid dropped from 58 in 1963 to 53 in 1966. By 1972 a plurality of 42 percent wanted economic aid to developing nations reduced, while only 7 percent wanted it increased. A plurality of 42 percent also wanted military aid to such allies as South Korea and Brazil reduced, while only 3 percent favored an increase.[24]

In the late 1960s and early 1970s many Americans also became disillusioned with the United Nations, which had enjoyed overwhelming public support during the Cold War. Those who believed that the U.N. was doing a poor job grew from 11 percent in 1961 to 43 percent (including 54 percent of the college educated) in 1971. Although support for the U.N. in 1972 was stronger than support for foreign aid, three times as many respondents favored reducing the American contribution to the U.N. as favored increasing it.[25]

During the Vietnam years many Americans soured on Presidential leadership in foreign policy and the national security establishment generally. The news media, which became much more aggressive in challenging official explanations than they had been prior to 1963, presented a succession of revelations which cast doubt on the credibility of American leaders. The government, many charged, had deliberately deceived the nation about the Gulf of Tonkin incident, covered up the My Lai massacre and other atrocities, and withheld information about American military activities in North Vietnam, Cambodia, and Laos. The Pentagon Papers, published in *The New York Times* and other newspapers in 1971, revealed repeated instances of deception in the development of Vietnam policy. Numerous books and articles published in the late 1960s and early 1970s sharply challenged both the direction of American foreign policy and the integrity of the nation's leaders.

In this climate of opinion the public came to doubt the credibility of Presidents Johnson and Nixon and to question the size of the military budget. When asked in October 1967, "Do you think the Johnson administration is or is not telling the public all they should know about the Vietnam war?", 70 percent said, "No." When asked the same question about the Nixon administration in 1971, 69 percent said, "No." In the early 1960s the public consistently supported increased defense expenditures; by 1969, however, 52 percent said that "too much" was being spent on defense, while only 8 percent said "too little." The belief that military expenditures were too high was strongest among the college educated and young people.[26]

These two groups, taken as a whole, had been strong supporters of American involvement in Vietnam in 1965 and 1966. But both had become largely disaffected by 1970. The disaffection ran deepest among college-educated youth, many of whom completely rejected the Cold War assumptions which college students in 1962 had supported in overwhelming numbers. A 1962 study found that 78 percent of male college students believed that the United States "must be willing to run any risk of war which may be necessary to prevent the spread of Communism." Ten years later only 22 percent agreed. To the statement, "The real enemy today is no longer Communism but rather war itself," 25 percent concurred in 1962 and 65 percent concurred in 1972.[27]

After interviewing in 1970 a sample of more than one hundred Americans aged 25–34 who had attended the "best" universities and who appeared to be headed toward top leadership positions, political scientist Graham T. Allison concluded that these young people almost unanimously rejected the Cold War assumptions that had dominated American policy for more than two decades. In addition to discounting Cold War rationales for policy, they doubted the credibility of America's leaders and believed that the United States as a nation was no more moral than other nations. Most important, with the exception of Vietnam they were more interested in domestic than in foreign policy problems. Although they believed that it was impossible as well as undesirable to return to the non-interventionism of the 1930s, they wanted "Vietnam over, defense budgets down, international entanglements cut." Allison concluded that the "Vietnam analogy" might be as important a guide for policy-makers in the 1970s and 1980s as the "Munich analogy" had been in the 1940s and 1950s.[28]

From July 1965 until June 1971, Americans viewed Vietnam as the "most important problem" facing the nation. The issue that finally superseded Vietnam in August 1971 was concern about the economy. This change was entirely appropriate, for inflation, unemployment, shortages, and other economic problems frequently dominated public debate in the ensuing years.[29]

The results of in-depth polls conducted in the fall of 1964 and in December 1974 suggested the extent of the shift of concern from international to domestic issues. In 1964 the five issues the respondents worried most about were all foreign policy issues: keeping the country out of war, combating world Communism, keeping America's defenses strong, preventing the use of nuclear weapons, and maintaining respect for the United States abroad. In 1974, in contrast, only 13 percent mentioned a foreign policy issue when asked to name the two or three most important problems which the federal government should be trying to solve. At a time when the rate of inflation exceeded 12 percent, it is not surprising that economic problems dominated the responses. Of the foreign policy problems mentioned, the five most important goals in 1974 were keeping peace in the world, protecting American security, securing adequate supplies of energy, protecting the jobs of American workers, and fostering international cooperation to solve common problems such as food, inflation, and energy.[30]

The experiences of the 1970s have made Americans recognize as never before the interrelatedness of the world economy, the fact that decisions made in one part of the world frequently have significant repercussions elsewhere. Grain sales to Russia have raised prices for American consumers, price hikes by the Organization of Petroleum Exporting Countries (OPEC) have contributed to worldwide inflation, and American manufacturers of such products as shoes, textiles, and steel have sought to limit imports, thereby protecting American jobs but jeopardizing employment in other nations. Trouble spots in the Middle East, in southern Africa, in Ireland, and in parts

1974: A brief encounter with dry gasoline pumps taught some Americans a lesson in global interdependence.

MacNelly in the Richmond *News Leader*

of Latin America have reminded Americans of the persistence of international problems, but concern about the domestic economy has been the most important factor in maintaining the attentive public's interest in foreign affairs in the 1970s.

The impact of economic issues on public perceptions of American foreign policy in the 1970s is illustrated by public reactions to events in the Middle East. Although American policy-makers and business leaders have been aware of the importance of Arab oil to the American economy since the 1940s, the general public from the 1940s through the 1960s viewed events in the Middle East either as part of the East-West struggle or as a bitter feud between the Arab states and Israel. The public supported actions to keep Communism out of the area, but it did not want the United States to become involved militarily in the Arab-Israeli conflict. Although most Americans sympathized with Israel, especially during the 1960s, the majority also believed that wars between the Arab states and Israel were virtually inevitable and that the

United States should send neither troops nor weapons to aid either side in the conflict.[31]

The Arab-Israeli conflict became more directly relevant to most Americans when the Arab oil-producing states imposed an embargo on the shipment of petroleum to the United States and other industrialized nations in the aftermath of the October 1973 war. Polls taken during the winter of 1974, when long lines at service stations popularized the term "energy crisis," showed that most Americans did not want to lessen support for Israel in order to restore the flow of oil from the Middle East. But most Americans did not support Israel uncritically. The public agreed with the statement that "Israel is friendly to the United States because it wants our military supplies" by a margin of 56 percent to 36 percent. A plurality also agreed that "Israel seems to feel the United States will back them up, no matter what they do." Although most Americans continued to support Israel and to dislike Palestinian leader Yasir Arafat, pollster Louis Harris wrote in 1975, "An Israel which appears to shun all peace efforts and boasts of its military power could well be told to find its backing elsewhere."[32]

Led by the American-Israel Public Affairs Committee, one of the most influential pressure groups operating on Capitol Hill in recent years, the pro-Israel lobby successfully worked for billions of dollars in aid to Israel during the mid-1970s. It also joined with labor unions and old-line Cold Warriors in frustrating efforts to move toward economic détente with the Soviet Union. The Nixon and Ford administrations, the Russians, and a growing number of American-based multinational corporations viewed closer economic ties as an integral feature of détente. The pro-Israel lobby, angry at the Soviet government's refusal to permit unrestricted emigration of Jews from Russia; the AFL-CIO, fearing that "exporting technology" to Russia and Eastern Europe would result in an eventual loss of jobs for American workers; and powerful Senators like Henry M. Jackson, trusting neither economic nor arms control agreements with Russia—all urged Congress to place restrictions on the increased trade with Russia advocated by those favoring détente. After years of disputes involving lobbyists favoring and opposing détente, the Congress, the administration, and the Russian government, all that could be said by 1977 was that trade with Russia had been less than administration officials and business leaders had hoped for, and that many American Jewish leaders continued to be dissatisfied with the Soviet government's treatment of Russian Jews.[33]

Disputes over Russian-American trade and the treatment of Russian Jews were only two of the obstructions to the achievement of détente with Russia, which public opinion polls showed was a highly popular goal after President Nixon's trip to Moscow in the spring of 1972. Conservative criticisms of the arms limitation agreements of 1972 and 1974, which often took the form of ominous warnings from groups like the Committee on the Present Danger that a new missile gap was going to develop, encouraged public mistrust. The views of Alexander Solzhenitsyn and other Russian dissidents were given extensive coverage in the mass media, as was Soviet support for left-wing elements in Portugal and Angola.[34]

Facing a serious challenge from conservative Ronald Reagan for the Republican nomination, President Ford in March 1976 dropped the word "détente" from his vocabulary. When President Carter in the first few months of his administration gave highest priority to human rights, the public generally approved, but Soviet leaders definitely did not. As 1977 ended, Americans appeared less hopeful than they had been five years before that a truly peaceful relationship between the two great nuclear powers could be established, but there was no indication that the public favored a return to the Cold War atmosphere of the early 1960s.

Favorable attitudes toward mainland China also appear to have peaked in the early 1970s. From April 1971, when an American table tennis team visited China, through Febru-

HIGH LOB

1972: The once formidable China lobby could not stop the Nixon-Kissinger "ping-pong diplomacy" and a new opening to China.

ary 1972, when Nixon became the first American President to visit China, mainland China was a leading subject in the mass media and at cocktail parties. Chinese fashions became stylish, and Chinese achievements in agriculture, education, and health care were stressed. The efforts of the greatly weakened China lobby and other conservative organizations to block moves toward détente with mainland China generally were ignored by both the news media and the Nixon Administration.

In announcing his upcoming visit to China in a nationwide television address on July 15, 1971, Nixon hailed his acceptance of Premier Chou En-lai's invitation as "a major development in our efforts to build a lasting peace in the world." His visit to China, much of which was broadcast on American television, suggested the beginning of a new era in Sino-American relations. The increasingly favorable attitudes toward mainland China beginning in the 1960s seemed to have culminated in steps leading inexorably toward normal diplomatic relations with Peking.[35]

As with relations with Russia, the hopes of the early 1970s have not been fulfilled. Although both trade and travel between the two nations have grown to modest levels, there has been little progress toward full diplomatic relations, which in Peking's view would require the ending of all American diplomatic and military ties with Taiwan. From early 1973 until Nixon's resignation in August 1974, public and official concentration on Watergate weakened the administration's ability to undertake new initiatives in foreign affairs; the Ford and Carter administrations placed a lower priority on China policy than the Nixon administration. Some liberal organizations have sought to mobilize support for making the necessary concessions, but the general public has shown little interest in the issue. The establishment of normal diplomatic relations with Peking now seems less imminent than it did when Nixon returned from China on February 28, 1972.

Because of Nixon's apparent success in dealing with Russia and China and his ending of direct American military involvement in Vietnam in January 1973, critics of Nixon's foreign policy tended to concentrate on strains in America's relations with Western Europe and Japan and on his failure to deal imaginatively with global concerns such as hunger and pollution. Popular among international businessmen and Democratic politicians in the 1970s has been "trilateralism," the idea that less emphasis needed to be placed on relations with Russia and China and more needed to be placed on relations with Western Europe and Japan. According to this view, the most important world problems increasingly were economic ones, and the three great industrial centers and trading partners needed to improve relations among themselves and adopt common strategies in dealing with challenges such as the one presented by the OPEC nations. President Carter, Secretary of State Cyrus Vance, National Security adviser

Zbigniew Brzezinski, and other officials were on the influential Trilateral Commission before taking office.[36]

Another important group of foreign policy activists, a group Brzezinski has called "planetary humanists," believed that the most important problems were neither East-West nor trilateral ones, but rather global in scope. In *World Without Borders* (1972), a major statement of this viewpoint, economist Lester R. Brown argued that problems such as environmental decay, world hunger, population growth, and the widening gap between rich and poor nations could only be solved by working toward the establishment of a world community. Instead of insisting that the United Nations be transformed into a world government, the planetary humanists emphasized the development of public awareness of belonging to a world community and the gradual building of institutions designed to deal with specific international problems such as pollution from oil tankers and the regulation of deep-sea mining. Among the groups stressing global interdependence were the Institute for World Order, the Overseas Development Council, the Ocean Education Project, and Bread for the World.[37]

The in-depth poll conducted in December 1974 suggested that, in theory at least, the general public agreed with most of the goals of both the trilateralists and the planetary humanists. Seventy-five percent said that it was "very important" that the United States have good relations with Western Europe, and 70 percent thought that maintaining good relations with Japan also was very important. Sixty-one percent said that combating world hunger should be a very important objective of American policy, and 79 percent favored giving economic aid if the United States could be sure that the aid actually was helping poor people in developing nations.[38]

Less heartening to the planetary humanists, but perhaps more revealing of public attitudes, was the finding that only 22 percent would be willing to pay 10 percent more for food in order to help nations with food shortages. And less than half believed that strengthening the United Nations or improving standards of living in developing nations was a very important goal for American policy.[39]

Although many planetary humanists hoped that the United States would take the lead in establishing a more equitable world order in the remaining quarter of the twentieth century, the fact was that by the mid-1970s the limits of America's ability to affect events outside its borders seemed painfully apparent. The Organization of Petroleum Exporting Countries set the world price of oil, a coalition of developing nations frequently passed resolutions in the U.N. General Assembly over explicit American opposition, and in the spring of 1975 the North Vietnamese and the Viet Cong finally won the Vietnam War. Despite several devaluations of the dollar which raised the price of foreign-made products, American industry faced increasing competition in consumer goods and even in basic commodities such as steel. Aided by persistent unemployment, protectionist sentiment seemed to be as strong in the late 1970s as at any time since the Great Depression.

Dismayed by economic difficulties, by Watergate, by the defeat in Indochina, and by revelations of CIA attempts to overthrow foreign governments and assassinate foreign leaders, the general public in the mid-1970s responded most enthusiastically to actions or rhetoric which seemed to promise the restoration of a sense of American honor. President Ford's swift military action against Cambodia in the *Mayaguez* affair in the summer of 1975 was popular, as was Reagan's insistence in the primaries in the spring of 1976 that the United States make no concessions in regard to the Panama Canal. And one of the most popular appeals of Jimmy Carter's successful campaign for the Presidency in 1976 was his call for the restoration to government of the high ideals of the American people. To achieve this end, he promised an open government, an administration which would keep the American people informed about foreign policy and respond to their opinions. If Carter does work toward this goal during his Presidency, the public's efforts to keep informed about foreign policy issues can help to restore a genuine sense of American honor.

6

WE THE PEOPLE
AND
OUR POLICY-MAKERS

American foreign policy acquires strength to
the extent that it is derived from competitive
discussion in front of a critical audience capable
of judgment and discrimination.

—GABRIEL A. ALMOND (1950) [1]

IN THE PRECEDING chapters I have concentrated on analyzing
the distribution of opinion in the general public, as reflected
primarily in public opinion polls, and the efforts of organizations to influence both public attitudes and official policy.
I also have argued that dominant assumptions affecting the
conduct of American policy have been established during
periods of broad public participation in foreign policy center-
ing on a specific, pressing issue: America's relationship to the
League of Nations, 1918–1920; the issue of involvement in
another world war, 1937–1941; the nature of the American
response to Communism, 1946–1952; and the foreign policy
implications of the Vietnam War and domestic unrest, 1965–
1972. In this concluding chapter I shall address two sets of
questions that in my judgment deserved separate consideration. Basically, the questions are these: What impact has the

public had on American foreign policy since 1918? And what have been some of the strengths and weaknesses of public involvement in the foreign policy process?

As political scientist V. O. Key, Jr. observed in 1961, "The sharp definition of the role of public opinion as it affects different kinds of policies under different types of situations presents an analytical problem of extraordinary difficulty." There are so many pressures affecting top policy-makers at any given time—information about events abroad, interpretations of those events within the administration and in Congress, signals coming from interest groups, the press, and the general public—that even a President or a Secretary of State might not be able to explain just what combination of factors influenced a particular decision. Did President Kennedy's decisions during the Cuban missile crisis, for example, derive more from his estimates of Russian intentions, from the interplay of ideas during his meetings with senior officials, or from his awareness of public pressures for a "firm" policy toward Cuba at a time when midterm Congressional elections were less than two weeks away? Although there are many useful clues to Kennedy's thinking, it may prove impossible to make a truly convincing analysis of the relative importance of the various factors influencing decision-making during the missile crisis. The analytical problem is compounded for the thousands of less dramatic decisions which every President makes.[2]

The difficulty in analyzing the role of public opinion in the formulation of policy is illustrated by the contradictory conclusions scholars have reached. Some have argued that modern American Presidents generally have been able to manipulate public opinion to support whatever policies they have wished to pursue. Others have emphasized constraints on policy-makers which are said to have prevented them from initiating constructive policies. By drawing general distinctions between public attitudes toward other nations and public attitudes toward wars, it is possible to clarify the manipulation-versus-constraint issue.[3]

The experience of the past sixty years suggests that public officials generally have been able to "educate" the majority of the American people in regard to attitudes toward particular foreign nations. The swings back and forth in attitudes toward Russia, for example, appear to have resulted more from well-publicized changes in official policy toward Russia than from changes inside Russia or alterations in Russian objectives in foreign policy. Since 1917 Russia has been Communist and it persistently has sought to expand its influence; yet the American government and public have alternated between extreme hostility, as in the late 1910s and late 1940s, and relative friendship, as in the early 1940s and early 1970s. Attitudes toward Japan, as William L. Neumann and others have suggested, also have tended to follow official policy. From 1931 through 1945, no other nation was viewed so consistently by both the government and the public as an enemy of the United States. Since World War II, the reality of economic, diplomatic, and military ties between the United States and Japan have helped to develop and sustain generally favorable attitudes. Finally, there can be no doubt that the Nixon administration's negotiations with the Peking government in the early 1970s resulted in a substantial shift in the direction of more favorable attitudes toward mainland China.[4]

Although the administration in power generally has been able to build the necessary public support for policies toward particular nations, all of the Presidents who have served during the four major wars in which America has become involved in this century have faced constraints from the public. Substantial public opposition to American membership in the League of Nations and to provisions of the Versailles treaty developed in the aftermath of World War I. Public opposition to involvement in another European war helped to defeat the Roosevelt administration's efforts to revise the neutrality laws in the spring of 1939. And public opinion turned sharply against the Presidents who decided upon large-scale American military involvement in Korea and Vietnam.

During the early years of the Vietnam War, President Johnson seemed to be able to command highly favorable reactions in the polls to whatever policies he chose to pursue. "The President makes public opinion, he does not follow it," sociologist Seymour Martin Lipset wrote in 1966. Two years later, public disgust with Johnson's handling of the war clearly contributed to the appeal of Senator Eugene McCarthy in the Democratic primaries and to Johnson's decision not to run for re-election. Although the nature and timing of the public constraints have varied, modern Presidents who have led the nation toward involvement in war ultimately have experienced constraints upon their leadership in foreign affairs.[5]

One important source of constraints has derived not from public pressures, but rather from assumptions about the role of public opinion in the American political system. Most American Presidents apparently have believed that, although they have the right and perhaps the duty to seek to build support for their policies, they should not make foreign policy decisions which are too far in advance of public opinion. "Looking back through American history," historian Ernest R. May has written, "one can almost count on one's fingers the numbers of occasions when American statesmen made major decisions that they thought contrary to the public will." [6]

To have an impact on foreign policy, the public does not have to rely on official sensitivity to polls and other indicators of public opinion. The mass public probably has its greatest effect on policy at the voting booth, whereas the much smaller attentive public tends to work through organizations which attempt to influence specific policies between elections. The voting booth is important not only because it permits the public to change the nation's leadership but also because elected officials continually must calculate which of many proposed policies are likely to win public approval. To take a current example, there may well be states in which a Senator's vote on the Panama Canal treaty might prove to be the margin of victory or defeat in the 1978 election.

A generally favorable evaluation of the administration's conduct of American foreign relations helped Wilson win re-election in 1916 and Roosevelt win an unprecedented third term in 1940, and public opinion polls suggest that it has been one of the most reliable indicators of probable success in Presidential elections ever since. The Democrats were viewed as the party which could best handle foreign affairs until the Korean War, the Republicans were the party best able to maintain peace throughout the 1950s, and then the Democrats led until 1966. Those who doubt the importance of foreign affairs in Presidential elections should be aware of how consistently the party which the general public has considered best able to end war or maintain peace has won the next election.[7]

Segments of the mass public have been most effective when they have held strong convictions on an issue. Substantial majorities of the voters in referenda in Massachusetts in the early 1930s supported American adherence to the World Court, and yet both Senators from the state voted against American adherence in February 1935. The Irish minority in Massachusetts strongly opposed any U.S. involvement with the court, whereas the majority generally was only mildly supportive. Similarly, the Kennedy administration, which had some desire to improve relations with mainland China, would have had to overcome bitter opposition from conservatives who believed that the United States should continue to ostracize the Peking government and stand firmly behind Chiang Kai-shek. As politicians know instinctively, retribution at the polls is much more likely to come from voters with strong convictions about an issue than from voters for whom an issue is relatively insignificant.

So many organizations have sought to influence American

1977: A 10,000-signature petition to Rep. Dewey Bartlett (R., Oklahoma) expressed patriotic wrath over the Panama treaties.

foreign policy over the past sixty years, and the apparent results have varied so greatly, that generalization is difficult. As emphasized in chapter 1, specific organizations have been much more influential at some times than at others. One can readily understand the frustration of many in the attentive public who have worked on foreign policy issues: not only is an organization's role in bringing about a favorable vote or administrative decision uncertain but there also is never any certainty of victory for one's cause. Even in losing, however, an organization might be helping to create changes both within the government and in public attitudes which might enable it to succeed in the future. Because the mass public remains apathetic about most foreign policy issues facing the government, there is always the possibility that foreign policy activists can tip the scales in favor of one policy or another.

And what of the strengths and weaknesses of public involvement in the foreign policy process? Has the experience

of the past sixty years justified the fears of such critics of
diplomacy by public opinion as George Kennan and Walter
Lippmann, or has it confirmed the faith of Woodrow Wilson
and George Gallup in the ultimate wisdom of the American
people? Does public involvement in foreign policy impede or
facilitate implementation of effective policies? Answers to
this final series of questions inevitably depend as much on
personal judgment as on historical analysis.

Public involvement in foreign policy appears to have
worked best—that is, facilitated the implementation of effective policies—on issues which both the public and officials
have had the background to assess intelligently. The area of
the world which American policy-makers consistently have
approached most effectively has been Western Europe, and
the public generally has supported initiatives such as Lend-
Lease and the Marshall Plan in dealing with the area. Most
Americans are descendants of Western Europeans, most have
studied the history and culture of Western Europe in schools
and colleges, and many have traveled in one or more Western
European nations. Newspaper wire services, magazines, and
radio and television networks have stationed a large percentage of their foreign correspondents in Western European
capitals. As we have seen, most Americans have viewed
Western Europeans as equals, and the American government
generally has treated their governments with respect. Although Americans tend to take them for granted, nations
predominantly European in background such as Canada,
Australia, and New Zealand also have been respected allies.

Americans generally have had fewer cultural ties with the
world's other major regions—Asia, Africa, Latin America,
and the Middle East. Very small percentages of Americans
have visited South America, Africa, or India, and very few
are fluent in Chinese, Japanese, Arabic, or Swahili. The
United States went to war in Indochina at a time when no
more than a few hundred Americans could be considered
experts on the history and culture of that region. Even today,

relatively few Americans could describe differences between Paraguay and Uruguay or between Iran and Iraq. Studies of textbooks used in American high schools have shown that coverage of such areas as Russia and the Middle East has been cursory at best and inaccurate at worst. Studies of newspaper coverage of Russia and Indochina have found that major developments frequently have been distorted or ignored even in quality newspapers like the *New York Times*.[8]

Public officials, who generally emerge from the same cultural background and read the same newspapers and periodicals as other attentive Americans, frequently have made decisions in dealing with such areas as Southeast Asia, Latin America, and the Middle East which could not have been made in regard to nations with which Americans were more familiar. The United States has assisted in overthrowing governments in each of these regions, it has sold or given large quantities of sophisticated weapons to nations with a record of unstable governments, and it has backed exile groups trying to gain power in nations such as Cuba and mainland China. Knowing little about these areas, the general public usually has acquiesced in governmental decisions made in the context of inadequate public debate until, as in the unusual case of Indochina, high casualty figures stirred debate and Americans began to conclude that their government's commitments had become too costly.

The difficulty of deciding in favor of the supporters or the critics of public involvement in foreign policy is illustrated by the efforts of ethnic groups to influence American policy. Members of ethnic organizations frequently have given needed economic assistance to those with whom they have identified abroad, and they also have alerted other Americans to serious violations of basic human rights. The persistent danger has been that some ethnic groups might place the desires of groups with which they have identified abroad ahead of consideration of the American national interest. American officials frequently have been faced with the dilemma of whether to pursue the national interest as they see it and risk the loss of votes in particular ethnic communities in the next election, or whether to yield to ethnic pressures and risk unwanted consequences abroad. In considering the continuing involvement of ethnic groups in foreign policy, it should not be forgotten that American assistance to bitterly anti-Castro Cuban refugees living in the United States contributed to serious tensions with Cuba in the early 1960s, tensions which culminated in a Soviet-American confrontation at the brink of nuclear war.[9]

An important change in the public's approach to foreign policy has been increased skepticism about the use of the all-purpose phrase "national security" to conceal information about foreign policy from public view. During World War II, elaborate systems were developed to conceal military information from German and Japanese agents. These systems were refined during the Cold War to keep information away from Russia and other Communist-bloc nations, but by the early 1960s some critics believed that the national security establishment was as interested in keeping embarrassing mistakes from the American people as it was in protecting legitimate secrets from the Russians. During the Cold War many Americans assumed that secrecy was essential to combat Communism. The experience of Vietnam and revelations of CIA activities undermined this assumption; by the late 1970s the belief that secrecy was necessary in the conduct of foreign affairs was offset by a growing belief in the people's right to know.

The Vietnam War also undermined the argument advanced so frequently in the 1950s and early 1960s that the public should leave foreign policy decisions to the "experts." If the experts could only produce policies which resulted in death and destruction in Indochina and divisiveness in American society, then perhaps the people—or at least the attentive public—should become even more involved in policy debates. Approached realistically, however, the experience of Vietnam did less to confirm the wisdom of the people than it did to discredit the foreign policy technicians who formulated Indochina policy during the 1950s and 1960s.

Another noteworthy change in the public's approach to foreign policy has been a decline in the instinctive belief in American superiority. "No country is more convinced than this one that she is right, or is more arrogant in her moral superiority," French journalist Raoul de Roussy de Sales wrote in 1942 while living in the United States. Sales believed that if the United States took an active role in world affairs after World War II, "it will be to impose her ideas, and she will consider her intervention a blessing for lost and suffering humanity." [10]

A statement by conservative columnist David Lawrence at the height of the Cold War a decade later seems to confirm Sales' premonition: "We must stop deluding ourselves with the idea of 'negotiating' with criminals. We must instead exalt morality. We cannot end tension merely by making a deal with the unmoral and the unscrupulous." The experience of Vietnam—especially the realization that Americans could make mistakes and commit atrocities—greatly undermined the assumption that the United States was inherently superior to other nations.[11]

Most Americans in the 1970s almost certainly feel less superior toward Russia than Lawrence and many others did in the 1950s, but the greatest change in attitudes toward other peoples probably has been toward Asians. The image of the "sneaky little Jap" of the 1930s and 1940s has been transformed into respect for Japan's economic prowess and stable democratic institutions. The industriousness of the Chinese under Communist rule has dispelled the stereotype of the "shiftless Chinaman." The belief in the inherent military superiority of the United States has been undermined by the stalemate and ultimate defeat by the determined North

Vietnamese and Viet Cong. And the recent defeat of Prime Minister Indira Gandhi surprised many who believed that democratic institutions meant nothing to most Indians.

Since World War II the public has been developing what Sheila K. Johnson has called "multiple images" to replace earlier stereotypes of Asians. It is important that Americans also continue to develop fuller, less ethnocentric images of Latin Americans, Africans, and Arabs.[12]

Perhaps the most hopeful development during the past sixty years has been the increased sophistication of large portions of the public in regard to foreign affairs. This has resulted from greater educational opportunities, more contacts with other peoples both directly and through media such as television, broader participation in foreign policy organizations, and experiences such as Vietnam. The declining belief in American superiority has been accompanied by the realization that other cultures are different and that they should not necessarily adopt American institutions and values.

As evidence of increased sophistication, I would cite the declining credibility of war slogans. Many educated Americans apparently believed that American involvement in World War I would indeed "make the world safe for democracy," and many also seemed to believe that the League of Nations could ensure permanent peace. During World War II many Americans believed, as William L. Neumann has observed, that "any future peace, to be a lasting one, had to be based on American ideals." But there was less interest than in World War I in making the war effort a crusade for the Four Freedoms or anything else. During the Korean and Vietnam wars, no slogans really caught on. General MacArthur insisted that there was no substitute for victory, but his popularity and the slogan that accompanied it declined rapidly soon after Truman fired him. President Johnson announced a Mekong River development project patterned after the Tennessee Valley Authority, but the public showed no enthusiasm for transferring American institutions and technology to Southeast Asia. Other nations, the public gradually had learned, could not be made over in America's image.[13]

From the perspective of the late 1970s, the most troubling feature of public involvement in foreign affairs is the fact that the generally increased sophistication has not encompassed international economics. Most Americans, including many of the college-educated, have no better understanding of economic relationships than did most Americans in the 1920s. The impact of multinational corporations, the role of trade in creating employment for some and contributing to unemployment for others, the growing dependence on other nations for resources such as oil—these and other issues generally are discussed in times of crisis or of scandal, but not in such a way as to educate large segments of the public. If the next series of international crises center on economic issues, the American people may be almost as ill-prepared to deal with these crises intelligently as they were to judge the merits of escalating the Vietnam War in 1965.

Another disturbing trend in the 1970s has been a widespread tendency to blame developing nations and international institutions for America's difficulties in world affairs. Strong criticisms of the developing nations' influence in the U.N. General Assembly and in other world bodies have become quite popular, as U.N. Ambassador Daniel Patrick Moynihan quickly learned. Many Americans also have found it convenient to blame other nations for U.S. economic difficulties: high oil prices and unfair competition in steel—not America's insatiable appetite for energy and antiquated steel mills—are viewed as the culprits. It is easy to overlook the successes of many U.N. agencies and of other international organizations such as the World Bank and the International Monetary Fund. It also is easy to blame economic difficulties on other nations and to ignore causes closer to home. In the profoundly interdependent world of the late twentieth century, however, Americans almost certainly will need to avoid the lure of strident nationalism and continue to support constructive steps toward increased international cooperation.

Primary responsibility for informing the public about the changing realities of international economics, the continuing importance of international institutions, and other foreign policy issues rests, as it has in the past, on four institutions: the federal government, foreign policy organizations, the educational system, and the mass media. Public confidence in the federal government was shaken severely during the decade from 1964 to 1974; official credibility on foreign policy is being restored gradually, but many Americans continue to be wary of pronouncements from Washington. Until a greater degree of mutual trust is achieved, the government's effectiveness in convincing the public of the importance of particular foreign policy issues will be impaired.

Although precise figures are not available, it is apparent that the number of Americans participating actively in foreign policy organizations is much smaller in the 1970s than it was in the 1950s. Some organizations active in the 1950s have declined, and others collapsed after the end of the Vietnam War. Although some organizations continue to conduct national programs, there is a need for the revitalization of local branches of national organizations. Without the stimulus provided by active local groups, and without the focus provided by a single overwhelming issue such as Vietnam, many even among the better educated tend to lose interest in foreign policy issues.

Because of the federal government's reduced effectiveness and the relatively small level of participation in foreign policy organizations, the greatest opportunity for public education in the near future lies with the educational system and the mass media, both of which could help substantially to make foreign affairs seem less foreign. The educational system at all levels needs to place considerably more emphasis than it has in the past on instruction in the history, culture, and contemporary problems of areas other than North America and

Western Europe. Students also need to develop at least a rudimentary understanding of international economics and the role of international institutions.

The mass media probably will continue to concentrate on entertainment, but public affairs coverage could be improved. Newspapers could present more front-page analyses of the context of contemporary issues, and magazines could present special issues on particular nations more frequently. Instead of focusing largely on foreign policy stories which involve controversy and violence, the commercial networks could present more stories on social conditions and public concerns within nations such as Japan and Brazil which seldom make the news. An excellent example of the potential of the electronic media is "All Things Considered," the evening news program on National Public Radio, which frequently features in-depth analysis of international issues. The mass media as a whole need to do as well in explaining the issues involved in particular situations as they do in presenting the partisan and other conflicting points of view in regard to possible solutions to world problems.

These suggestions are not intended as panaceas; nor do I wish to overlook the resistance of large segments of the public to learning about international issues. The fact is that American foreign policy has gone astray not when the mass public was uninformed, which has been most of the time, but when most public officials and members of the attentive public have known little about an issue or region of the world. American ignorance about Asia has been the most costly over the past sixty years, but there also have been times when ignorance of Latin America, Africa, the Middle East, and Russia have created dangers greater than particular situations warranted.

Whether or not an effort to revitalize local foreign policy groups and improve the handling of international issues in the schools and in the media would have much effect on the mass public, it almost certainly would assist the attentive public and the policy-makers selected from that group. These foreign policy activists formulate American policy and shape the basic framework of public reactions to it. So long as the formulation of policy meets Almond's test of "competitive discussion in front of a critical audience capable of judgment and discrimination," there can be increased confidence in the conduct of American foreign policy.

NOTES

CHAPTER 1

1. Quoted in Bernard Berelson and Morris Janowitz, eds., *Reader in Public Opinion and Communication*. 2d ed. rev. (New York: Free Press, 1966), p. 7.
2. M. Brewster Smith, Jerome S. Bruner, and Robert W. White, *Opinions and Personality* (New York: Wiley, 1956), pp. 2–5.
3. Alfred O. Hero, Jr., *Americans and World Affairs* (Boston: World Peace Foundation, 1959), pp. 21–32; Martin Kriesberg, "Dark Areas of Ignorance," in Lester Markel, ed., *Public Opinion and Foreign Policy* (New York: Harper and Bros., 1949), p. 56.
4. John E. Mueller, *War, Presidents and Public Opinion* (New York: Wiley, 1973), pp. 122–25.
5. *Gallup Opinion Index*, no. 57 (March 1970), p. 15.
6. Robert S. Lynd and Helen Merrell Lynd, *Middletown in Transition: A Study in Cultural Conflicts* (New York: Harcourt, Brace & Co., 1937), p. 386; Paul F. Lazarsfeld and Harry Field, *The People Look at Radio* (Chapel Hill: University of North Carolina Press, 1946), p. 43; *Media and Non-Media Effects on the Formation of Public Opinion* (Washington, D.C.: American Institute for Political Communication, 1969), p. 44.
7. Robert K. Merton, *Social Theory and Social Structure*, 3rd ed. rev. (New York: Free Press, 1968), pp. 451–52; Hero, *Americans and World Affairs*, pp. 107–9.
8. George Belknap and Angus Campbell, "Political Party Iden-

tification and Attitudes Toward Foreign Policy," *Public Opinion Quarterly* 15 (Winter 1951–52), pp. 605–8; Mueller, *War, Presidents and Public Opinion*, pp. 270–71.

 9. Belknap and Campbell, "Political Party Identification and Attitudes Toward Foreign Policy," pp. 614–15, 621.

10. Louis L. Gerson, *The Hyphenate in Recent American Politics and Diplomacy* (Lawrence: University of Kansas Press, 1964), p. 3.

11. Because of the difficulty of identifying direct religious influences on public opinion, and because of the impreciseness of the categories "Protestant," "Catholic," and "Jew," the least informative of Alfred O. Hero, Jr.'s many works on public opinion and foreign policy is *American Religious Groups View Foreign Policy, 1937–1969* (Durham: Duke University Press, 1973).

12. Edward W. Chester, *Sectionalism, Politics, and American Diplomacy* (Metuchen, N.J.: Scarecrow Press, 1975), pp. 187–226.

13. Gabriel A. Almond, *The American People and Foreign Policy* (New York: Harcourt, Brace, 1950), pp. 122–27; Ralph B. Levering, *American Opinion and the Russian Alliance, 1939–1945* (Chapel Hill: University of North Carolina Press, 1976), pp. 128–29.

14. Bernard C. Cohen, "Mass Communication and Foreign Policy," in James N. Rosenau, ed., *Domestic Sources of Foreign Policy* (New York: Free Press, 1967), p. 196.

15. Dorothy Detzer, *Appointment on the Hill* (New York: Holt, 1948), pp. 59–60.

16. *Opinion News*, vol. 3, no. 10 (Nov. 7, 1944), p. 6; Hadley Cantril and Mildred Strunk, *Public Opinion, 1935–1946* (Princeton: Princeton University Press, 1951), p. 265.

17. Bernard C. Cohen, *The Press and Foreign Policy* (Princeton: Princeton University Press, 1963), p. 251; Alfred O. Hero, Jr., *The Southerner and World Affairs* (Baton Rouge: Louisiana State University Press, 1965), p. 45.

18. Smith, Bruner, and White, *Opinions and Personality*, p. 64; Karl W. Deutsch and Richard L. Merritt, "Effects of Events on National and International Images," in Herbert C. Kelman, ed., *International Behavior* (New York: Holt, Rinehart, and

Winston, 1965), p. 146; Walter Lippmann, *Public Opinion* (New York: Free Press, 1965), pp. 54–55.

19. Mueller, *War, Presidents and Public Opinion*, pp. 1–19; Michael Wheeler, *Lies, Damn Lies, and Statistics: The Manipulation of Public Opinion in America* (New York: Norton, 1976), p. 293 and *passim*.

20. Bernard C. Cohen, *The Public's Impact on Foreign Policy* (Boston: Little, Brown, 1973), p. 195; Raymond A. Bauer, Ithiel de Sola Pool, and Lewis A. Dexter, *American Business and Public Policy: The Politics of Foreign Trade* (New York: Atherton Press, 1967), p. 398.

21. The Commission on Freedom of the Press, *A Free and Responsible Press* (Chicago: University of Chicago Press, 1947), p. 55; Adnan Almaney, "International and Foreign Affairs on Network Television News," *Journal of Broadcasting* 14 (Fall 1970), pp. 499–509; Benjamin D. Singer, "Violence, Protest, and War in TV News," *Public Opinion Quarterly* 34 (Winter 1970–71), pp. 613–16.

CHAPTER 2

1. Allen W. Dulles and Hamilton Fish Armstrong, *Can We Be Neutral?* (New York: Harper and Row, 1936), pp. 44–45.

2. Charles W. Smith, Jr., *Public Opinion in a Democracy* (New York: Prentice-Hall, 1939), p. 518.

3. Mark Sullivan, *Our Times, 1900–1925*, VI (New York: Charles Scribner's Sons, 1935), p. 4.

4. Peter G. Filene, *Americans and the Soviet Experiment, 1917–1933* (Cambridge: Harvard University Press, 1967), pp. 9–63; Christopher Lasch, *The American Liberals and the Russian Revolution* (New York: Columbia University Press, 1962), *passim*.

5. Warren F. Kuehl, *Seeking World Order: The United States and International Organization to 1920* (Nashville: Vanderbilt University Press, 1969), pp. 298–314; Arthur S. Link, *Wilson the Diplomatist* (Baltimore: Johns Hopkins Press, 1957), pp. 127–39.

6. James J. Lancaster, "The Protestant Churches and the Fight for Ratification of the Versailles Treaty," *Public Opinion*

Quarterly 31 (Winter 1967–68), pp. 599–619; Robert Moats Miller, "The Attitudes of the Major Protestant Churches in America Toward War and Peace, 1919–1929," *The Historian* 19 (November 1956), pp. 15–23.

7. Edward W. Chester, *Sectionalism, Politics, and American Diplomacy* (Metuchen, N.J.: Scarecrow Press, 1975), pp. 178–79.

8. George Bradford Neumann, *A Study of International Attitudes of High School Students* (New York: Teachers College, Columbia University, 1926), pp. 46–48; Chester, *Sectionalism, Politics, and American Diplomacy*, p. 195.

9. Robert S. Lynd and Helen Merrell Lynd, *Middletown: A Study in American Culture* (New York: Harcourt, Brace, and World, 1929), pp. 482–83, 489; Robert S. Lynd and Helen Merrell Lynd, *Middletown in Transition: A Study in Cultural Conflicts* (New York: Harcourt, Brace, and World, 1937), p. 383; Paul W. Penningroth, "Cityville: A Study of Public Opinion on International Affairs," mimeo. (New York: American Community, 1930), pp. 77–78; Sinclair Lewis, *Babbitt* (New York: Harcourt, Brace, and World, 1922), *passim*.

10. Robert A. Divine, *American Immigration Policy, 1924–1952* (New Haven: Yale University Press, 1957), pp. 14–23; Eleanor Tupper and George E. McReynolds, *Japan in American Opinion* (New York: Macmillan, 1937), pp. 188–91.

11. Ray H. Abrams, *Preachers Present Arms* (Scottdale, Pa.: Herald Press, 1969), pp. 234–39; Charles Chatfield, *For Peace and Justice: Pacifism in America, 1914–1941* (Knoxville: University of Tennessee Press, 1971), pp. 125–29.

12. Michael L. Kammen, ed., *"What Is the Good of History?" Selected Letters of Carl L. Becker, 1900–1945* (Ithaca: Cornell University Press, 1973), pp. 119–20.

13. C. Leonard Hoag, *Preface to Preparedness: The Washington Disarmament Conference and Public Opinion* (Washington, D.C.: American Council on Foreign Affairs, 1941), pp. 74–123; Roger Dingman, *Power in the Pacific: The Origins of Naval Arms Limitation, 1914–1922* (Chicago: University of Chicago Press, 1976), pp. 212–13.

14. Dorothy Detzer, *Appointment on the Hill* (New York: Holt, 1948), p. 101.

15. Chester, *Sectionalism, Politics, and American Diplomacy,* p. 196.
16. Hamilton Fish Armstrong, *Peace and Counterpeace: From Wilson to Hitler* (New York: Harper and Row, 1971), p. 196; *Fifty Years: The Story of the Foreign Policy Association, 1918–1968* (New York: Foreign Policy Association, 1968), p. 7.
17. Joan Hoff Wilson, *American Business and Foreign Policy, 1920–1933* (Lexington: University Press of Kentucky, 1971), p. xvi.
18. Filene, *Americans and the Soviet Experiment,* p. 266.
19. H. V. Kaltenborn, *We Look at the World* (New York: Rae D. Henkle, 1930), pp. 40–58.
20. Gabriel A. Almond, *The American People and Foreign Policy* (New York: Harcourt, Brace, 1950), p. 73; Thomas A. Bailey, *The Man in the Street* (New York: Macmillan, 1948), p. 119.
21. Philip C. Jessup, *International Security: The American Role in Collective Action for Peace* (New York: Council on Foreign Relations, 1935), p. 70; Denna F. Fleming, *The United States and the World Court* (Garden City, N.Y.: Doubleday, 1955), p. 129.
22. Robert A. Divine, *The Illusion of Neutrality* (Chicago: University of Chicago Press, 1962), pp. 77–85.
23. John E. Wiltz, *In Search of Peace: The Senate Munitions Inquiry, 1934–36* (Baton Rouge: Louisiana State University Press, 1963), pp. 20–25, 224–31.
24. John W. Masland, "The 'Peace' Groups Join Battle," *Public Opinion Quarterly* 4 (December 1940), p. 668; Dulles and Armstrong, *Can We Be Neutral?,* pp. 97, 118–19.
25. Tupper and McReynolds, *Japan in American Opinion,* pp. 331–37.
26. *Ibid.,* pp. 327–30.
27. William L. Neumann, *America Encounters Japan: From Perry to MacArthur* (Baltimore: Johns Hopkins Press, 1963), pp. 222–27.
28. *Ibid.,* pp. 215, 222, 258.
29. Arnold A. Offner, *American Appeasement: United States Foreign Policy and Germany, 1933–1938* (Cambridge: Harvard University Press, 1969), pp. 1–13; Eugene H. Bacon, "Ameri-

can Press Opinion of Hitler, 1932–1937," (Unpub. M.A. thesis, Georgetown University, 1949), pp. 214–15.

30. Offner, *American Appeasement*, pp. 60–63.
31. *Ibid.*, pp. 82–83.
32. *Ibid.*, pp. 86–88.
33. Bacon, "American Press Opinion of Hitler," p. 214.
34. John P. Diggins, *Mussolini and Fascism: The View from America* (Princeton: Princeton University Press, 1972), pp. 24–39.
35. *Ibid.*, pp. 302–5; Divine, *Illusion of Neutrality*, pp. 150–51.
36. Robert G. Weisbord, *Ebony Kinship: Africa, Africans, and the Afro-American* (Westport, Conn.: Greenwood Press, 1973), pp. 96–102.
37. Diggins, *Mussolini and Fascism*, pp. 289– 302.

CHAPTER 3

1. Quoted in Edwin Borchard and William Potter Lage, *Neutrality for the United States* (New Haven: Yale University Press, 1940), p. 352.
2. George Q. Flynn, *Roosevelt and Romanism: Catholics and American Diplomacy, 1937–1945* (Westport, Conn.: Greenwood Press, 1976), pp. 47–54.
3. George H. Gallup, *The Gallup Poll, 1935–1971* (New York: Random House, 1972), I, p. 132; Alfred O. Hero, Jr., *American Religious Groups View Foreign Policy, 1937–1969* (Durham: Duke University Press, 1973), p. 22.
4. Quoted in Michael Leigh, *Mobilizing Consent: Public Opinion and American Foreign Policy, 1937–1947* (Westport, Conn.: Greenwood Press, 1976), p. 21.
5. Manfred Jonas, *Isolationism in America, 1935–1941* (Ithaca: Cornell University Press, 1966), pp. 32–70.
6. Mark Lincoln Chadwin, *The Hawks of World War II* (Chapel Hill: University of North Carolina Press, 1968), p. 277.
7. Robert A. Divine, *The Reluctant Belligerent: American Entry Into World War II* (New York: Wiley, 1965), p. 45; Selig Adler, *The Uncertain Giant, 1921–1941* (New York: Macmillan, 1965), pp. 190–91.
8. Gallup, *The Gallup Poll*, I, pp. 120, 154.

9. *Ibid.*, pp. 71, 84, 90, 131–32.
10. *Ibid.*, pp. 121, 125, 130, 131.
11. *Ibid.*, pp. 154, 178, 183, 188.
12. *Ibid.*, pp. 222–31; Walter Johnson, *The Battle Against Isolation* (Chicago: University of Chicago Press, 1944), pp. 85–113.
13. Gallup, *The Gallup Poll*, I, pp. 226, 231; Chadwin, *The Hawks of World War II*, p. 280.
14. Gallup, *The Gallup Poll*, I, pp. 224, 252, 276, 282; Raoul de Roussy de Sales, *The Making of Yesterday* (New York: Reynal & Hitchcock, 1947), p. 192.
15. Gallup, *The Gallup Poll*, I, pp. 256, 296, 311.
16. *Ibid.*, p. 339; Harry H. Field, "American Public Opinion and Foreign Policy," mimeo. (New York: American Council of the Institute of Pacific Relations, 1945), p. 28.
17. Gallup, *The Gallup Poll*, I, p. 339; William A. Lydgate, *What America Thinks* (New York: Crowell, 1944), p. 57.
18. Gallup, *The Gallup Poll*, I, p. 499.
19. Lydgate, *What America Thinks*, pp. 52–53; Harry H. Field and Louise M. Van Patten, "If the American People Made the Peace," *Public Opinion Quarterly* 8 (Winter 1944–45), p. 510.
20. Gallup, *The Gallup Poll*, I, pp. 477, 483, 521.
21. *Ibid.*, p. 507.
22. *Ibid.*, pp. 405–7, 411; "The Fortune Survey," *Fortune* 29 (March 1944), p. 94.
23. Kenneth E. Shewmaker, *Americans and Chinese Communists, 1927–1945* (Ithaca: Cornell University Press, 1971), pp. 239–346.
24. Warren B. Walsh, "American Attitudes toward Russia," *Antioch Review* 7 (June 1947), pp. 183–89; Ralph B. Levering, *American Opinion and the Russian Alliance, 1939–1945* (Chapel Hill: University of North Carolina Press, 1976), pp. 39–199.
25. Arthur H. Vandenberg, Jr., ed., *The Private Papers of Senator Vandenberg* (Boston: Houghton Mifflin, 1952), p. 1.
26. Robert A. Divine, *Second Chance: The Triumph of Internationalism in America During World War II* (New York: Atheneum, 1967), pp. 36–37, 98–103.

27. *Ibid.*, pp. 127–28, 141–47; Leigh, *Mobilizing Consent*, pp. 117–32.

28. Field and Van Patten, "If the American People Made the Peace," p. 503; Gallup, *The Gallup Poll*, I, pp. 340, 451–52, 497.

29. William A. Scott and Stephen B. Withey, *The United States and the United Nations: The Public View, 1945–1955* (New York: Carnegie Endowment for International Peace, 1958), pp. 11–13.

30. John Morton Blum, *V Was for Victory: Politics and American Culture During World War II* (New York: Harcourt, Brace, Jovanovich, 1976), p. 304.

31. Lydgate, *What America Thinks*, pp. 60–62.

32. Gallup, *The Gallup Poll*, I, pp. 393–94.

33. Henry R. Luce, "America's War and America's Peace," *Life* 12 (16 February 1942), p. 85; Cordell Hull, *The Memoirs of Cordell Hull* (New York: Macmillan, 1948), II, pp. 1314–15.

34. Samuel I. Rosenman, ed., *The Public Papers and Addresses of Franklin D. Roosevelt* (New York: Random House, 1950), XIII, p. 586.

CHAPTER 4

1. "Public Thinking about Atomic Warfare and Civil Defense" (University of Michigan, Survey Research Center, 1950), pp. 1–2. Italics in original.

2. Ernest R. May, *"Lessons" of the Past: The Use and Misuse of History in American Foreign Policy* (New York: Oxford University Press, 1973), pp. 19–51.

3. Gallup, *The Gallup Poll*, I, pp. 576, 673, 736; II, pp. 1028, 1104.

4. Gallup, *The Gallup Poll*, I, pp. 525, 587, 736; II, pp. 839, 888.

5. *Ibid.*, pp. 567, 581–82, 682; "Attitudes toward United States–Russian Relations, October, 1948" (University of Michigan, Survey Research Center, 1948), p. ii; John Lewis Gaddis, *The United States and the Origins of the Cold War, 1941–1947* (New York: Columbia University Press, 1972), pp. 282–315.

6. Gallup, *The Gallup Poll*, I, pp. 721, 759.

7. Gallup, *The Gallup Poll*, I, pp. 653, 719, 723; II, pp. 791–92, 794; E. Raymond Wilson, *Uphill for Peace: Quaker Impact on Congress* (Richmond, Indiana: Friends United Press, 1975), p. 19; Lawrence S. Wittner, *Rebels Against War: The American Peace Movement, 1941–1960* (New York: Columbia University Press, 1969), pp. 162–64.

8. Theodore A. Wilson, *The Marshall Plan, 1947–1951* (New York: Foreign Policy Association, 1977), p. 36.

9. Gallup, *The Gallup Poll*, I, p. 637; II, p. 815; "Public Attitudes toward American Foreign Policy" (University of Michigan, Survey Research Center, 1947), p. ii.

10. Gallup, *The Gallup Poll*, I, pp. 584, 686–7.

11. Herzel Fishman, *American Protestantism and a Jewish State* (Detroit: Wayne State University Press, 1973), pp. 72–82.

12. John Snetsinger, *Truman, the Jewish Vote, and the Creation of Israel* (Stanford, Calif.: Hoover Institution Press, 1974), pp. 4–140.

13. Gallup, *The Gallup Poll*, I, pp. 728, 773–74; II, pp. 818, 831, 852.

14. Gallup, *The Gallup Poll*, II, pp. 868, 915.

15. *Ibid.*, pp. 942–93; John E. Mueller, *War, Presidents and Public Opinion* (New York: Wiley, 1973), p. 270.

16. Gallup, *The Gallup Poll*, II, pp. 939, 942, 970; Mueller, *War, Presidents and Public Opinion*, p. 270.

17. Mueller, *War, Presidents and Public Opinion*, pp. 270, 272.

18. Gallup, *The Gallup Poll*, II, pp. 969, 981, 993, 998.

19. *Ibid.*, pp. 971, 984, 995–96.

20. *Ibid.*, pp. 962, 968; Mueller, *War, Presidents and Public Opinion*, p. 40

21. Gallup, *The Gallup Poll*, II, pp. 962, 964, 998–99.

22. Stanley D. Bachrak, *The Committee of One Million: "China Lobby" Politics, 1953–1971* (New York: Columbia University Press, 1976), pp. 62–151.

23. Louis L. Gerson, *The Hyphenate in Recent American Politics and Diplomacy* (Lawrence: University of Kansas Press, 1964), p. 190.

24. John P. Diggins, *Up from Communism: Conservative Odysseys in American Intellectual History* (New York: Harper & Row, 1975), pp. 331–37; Barry Goldwater, *The Conscience of a*

Conservative (New York: Hillman Books, 1960), p. 92. Italics in original.

25. Grenville Clark and Louis B. Sohn, *World Peace Through World Law* (Cambridge: Harvard University Press, 1958), p. xxxii; Jon A. Yoder, "The United World Federalists: Liberals for Law and Order," in Charles Chatfield, ed., *Peace Movements in America* (New York: Schocken Books, 1973), p. 105.

26. Bachrak, *The Committee of One Million*, pp. 163–64; Edwin N. Hiebert, *The Impact of Atomic Energy* (Newton, Kansas: Faith and Life Press, 1961), pp. 204–65.

27. Gallup, *The Gallup Poll*, II, pp. 1142, 1226, 1304, 1320–21, 1435, 1444, 1460, 1488, 1554; III, pp. 1700, 1726, 1734, 1738.

28. *Ibid.*, II, pp. 1277, 1309; III, pp. 1655, 1699, 1754, 1799.

29. *Ibid.*, II, pp. 1172, 1326–27, 1347, 1528; III, p. 1596.

30. *Ibid.*, II, pp. 1347, 1374.

31. Edgar M. Bottome, *The Missile Gap* (Rutherford, N.J.: Fairleigh Dickinson University Press, 1971), p. 80.

32. Gallup, *The Gallup Poll*, III, pp. 1600, 1729–30, 1734–35.

33. *Ibid.*, II, pp. 1146, 1236.

34. *Ibid.*, II, pp. 1191, 1455; III, pp. 1721, 1787.

35. *Ibid.*, III, pp. 1672, 1712, 1717; Arthur M. Schlesinger, Jr., *The Imperial Presidency* (Boston: Houghton Mifflin, 1973).

36. Gallup, *The Gallup Poll*, III, pp. 1743, 1753, 1759.

CHAPTER 5

1. Michael Parenti, *The Anti-Communist Impulse* (New York: Random House, 1969), pp. 7–8.

2. J. William Fulbright, *Old Myths and New Realities* (New York: Random House, 1964), p. 128; Richard D. Challener, "The Next President's Foreign Policy Legacy," *University—A Princeton Quarterly*, no. 69 (Summer 1976), pp. 11–12.

3. Gallup, *The Gallup Poll*, III, pp. 1799, 1837, 1847, 1949; *New York Post*, March 25, 1965.

4. Gallup, *The Gallup Poll*, III, p. 1797; Lloyd A. Free and Hadley Cantril, *The Political Beliefs of Americans* (New York: Simon and Schuster, 1968), p. 92.

5. Bennett Korvig, *The Myth of Liberation* (Baltimore: Johns Hopkins Press, 1973), pp. 252, 257; American Bar Association, Standing Committee on Education Against Communism, *Peaceful Coexistence: A Communist Blueprint for Victory* (Chicago: American Bar Association, 1964).

6. Gallup, *The Gallup Poll*, III, pp. 1942, 1976; *New York Post*, July 7, 1965.

7. Gallup, *The Gallup Poll*, III, pp. 1808, 2107.

8. A. J. Steele, *The American People and China* (New York: McGraw-Hill, 1966), pp. 130–35, 163–73.

9. Gallup, *The Gallup Poll*, III, pp. 1811, 1881, 2053; Free and Cantril, *The Political Beliefs of Americans*, p. 89.

10. Steele, *The American People and China*, p. 266; Gallup, *The Gallup Poll*, III, pp. 1981, 2183.

11. Steele, *The American People and China*, pp. 266–67.

12. *Ibid.*, p. 200.

13. John E. Mueller, *War, Presidents and Public Opinion* (New York: Wiley, 1973), pp. 54–55.

14. *Ibid.*, pp. 85–97; Robert Weissberg, *Public Opinion and Popular Government* (Englewood Cliffs, N.J.: Prentice-Hall, 1976), pp. 143–53.

15. Gallup, *The Gallup Poll*, III, pp. 1958, 2008, 2013.

16. Mueller, *War, Presidents and Public Opinion*, pp. 116–41.

17. *Ibid.*, p. 166; Harold E. Quinley, "The Protestant Clergy and the War in Vietnam," *Public Opinion Quarterly* 34 (Spring 1970), p. 46.

18. Ray H. Abrams, *Preachers Present Arms* (Scottdale, Pa.: Herald Press, 1969), p. 282.

19. Irwin Unger, *The Movement: A History of the American New Left, 1959–1972* (New York: Dodd, Mead, 1974), p. 193; William L. O'Neill, *Coming Apart: An Informal History of America in the 1960's* (New York: Quadrangle, 1971), p. 405.

20. For suggestions from three antiwar social scientists that peace workers should be concerned about personal appearance and take other steps to improve their effectiveness, see Milton J. Rosenberg, Sidney Verba, and Philip E. Converse, *Vietnam and the Silent Majority: The Dove's Guide* (New York: Harper & Row, 1970), pp. 142–54.

21. Albert H. Cantril and Charles W. Roll, Jr., *Hopes and Fears of the American People* (New York: Universe Books, 1971), p. 12.
22. Gallup, *The Gallup Poll*, III, p. 2183.
23. William Watts and Lloyd A. Free, eds., *State of the Nation* New York: Universe Books, 1973), pp. 200–1, 204.
24. *Ibid.*, pp. 218–19; Gallup, *The Gallup Poll*, III, pp. 1802, 1995.
25. Gallup, *The Gallup Poll*, III, pp. 1735, 2329; Watts and Free, *State of the Nation*, p. 218.
26. Hazel Erskine, "The Polls: Government Information Policy," *Public Opinion Quarterly* 35 (Winter 1971–72), pp. 644–45, 646; Gallup, *The Gallup Poll*, III, pp. 2210, 2298.
27. Roger B. Handberg, Jr., "The 'Vietnam Analogy': Student Attitudes on War," *Public Opinion Quarterly* 36 (Winter 1972–73), p. 613.
28. Graham T. Allison, "Cool It: The Foreign Policy of Young America," *Foreign Policy* 1 (Winter 1970–71), pp. 148–60.
29. Gallup, *The Gallup Poll*, III, pp. 1944, 1957, 1973, 1979, 2009, 2026, 2090, 2107, 2151, 2180, 2252–53, 2268, 2292, 2311.
30. Free and Cantril, *The Political Beliefs of Americans*, p. 52; John E. Rielly, ed., *American Public Opinion and U.S. Foreign Policy 1975* (Chicago: Chicago Council on Foreign Relations, 1975), pp. 10–13.
31. Gallup, *The Gallup Poll*, III, pp. 2149–50, 2181; Robert H. Trice, *Interest Groups and the Foreign Policy Process: U.S. Policy in the Middle East* (Beverly Hills, Calif.: Russell Sage Foundation, 1976), p. 30.
32. Louis Harris, "Oil or Israel?" *New York Times Magazine*, 6 April 1975, p. 34.
33. Russell Warren Howe and Sarah Hays Trott, *The Power Peddlers: How Lobbyists Mold America's Foreign Policy* (Garden City, N.Y.: Doubleday, 1977), pp. 225–67.
34. *Washington Post*, June 27, 1972, and March 18, 1977; Charles Gati and Tobi Trister Gati, *The Debate over Détente* (New York: Foreign Policy Association, 1977), pp. 14–54.
35. Kwan Ha Yim, *China and the U.S., 1964–72* (New York:

Facts on File, 1975), pp. 219–43; *New York Post*, November 6, 1971; *Washington Post*, March 12, 1972.

36. Zbigniew Brzezinski, "U.S. Foreign Policy: The Search for Focus," *Foreign Affairs* 51 (July 1973), pp. 716–23.

37. *Ibid.*, p. 712; Lester R. Brown, *World Without Borders* (New York: Random House, 1972), pp. 15–154, 301–64.

38. Rielly, *American Public Opinion and U.S. Foreign Policy 1975*, pp. 13, 21, 27.

39. *Ibid.*, pp. 13, 26.

CHAPTER 6

1. Gabriel A. Almond, *The American People and Foreign Policy* (New York: Harcourt, Brace, 1950), pp. 145–46.

2. V. O. Key, Jr., *Public Opinion and American Democracy* (New York: Knopf, 1961), p. 7.

3. For a more detailed discussion of the contrasting positions, see Michael Leigh, *Mobilizing Consent: Public Opinion and American Foreign Policy, 1937–1947* (Westport, Conn.: Greenwood Press, 1976), pp. xiii–xvi, 167–71.

4. William L. Neumann, *America Encounters Japan: From Perry to MacArthur* (Baltimore: Johns Hopkins Press, 1963), p. 305; Akira Iriye, "Introduction," in Iriye, ed., *Mutual Images: Essays in American-Japanese Relations* (Cambridge: Harvard University Press, 1975), p. 15.

5. Quoted in Charles W. Roll, Jr., and Albert H. Cantril, *Polls: Their Use and Misuse in Politics* (New York: Basic Books, 1972), p. 146.

6. Ernest R. May, "An American Tradition in Foreign Policy: The Role of Public Opinion," in William H. Nelson, ed., *Theory and Practice in American Politics* (Chicago: University of Chicago Press, 1966), p. 117.

7. Gallup, *The Gallup Poll*, I, p. 687; II, pp. 1249, 1383, 1405, 1492, 1566; III, pp. 1632, 1666, 1677–78, 1803, 1817, 1868, 1904, 2018, 2167, 2264.

8. William J. Griswold and others, *The Image of the Middle East in Secondary School Textbooks* (New York: Middle East Association of North America, 1976), pp. 22–27; Richard W.

Burkhardt, "The Soviet Union in American School Textbooks," *Public Opinion Quarterly* 11 (Winter 1947–48), pp. 569–71; Martin Kriesberg, "Soviet News in the 'New York Times,'" *Public Opinion Quarterly* 10 (Winter 1946–47), pp. 540–64; George Stanley Turnbull, Jr., "Reporting of the War in Indochina: A Critique," *Journalism Quarterly* 34 (Winter 1957), pp. 87–89.

9. Louis L. Gerson, *The Hyphenate in Recent American Politics and Diplomacy* (Lawrence: University of Kansas Press, 1964), p. 21; George F. Kennan, *The Cloud of Danger: Current Realities of American Foreign Policy* (Boston: Little, Brown, 1977), pp. 6–7.

10. Raoul de Roussy de Sales, *The Making of Yesterday* (New York: Reynal & Hitchcock, 1947), p. 259.

11. Quoted in Joseph Barber, ed., *Diplomacy and the Communist Challenge* (New York: Council on Foreign Relations, 1954), p. 39.

12. Sheila K. Johnson, *American Attitudes toward Japan, 1941–1975* (Washington, D.C.: AEI-Hoover Press, 1975), p. 114.

13. William L. Neumann, *After Victory: Churchill, Roosevelt, Stalin and the Making of the Peace* (New York: Harper & Row, 1967), p. 32.

SELECTED
BIBLIOGRAPHY

Adler, Selig. *The Isolationist Impulse.* New York: Abelard-Schuman, 1957.

Almond, Gabriel A. *The American People and Foreign Policy.* New York: Harcourt, Brace, 1950.

Bachrak, Stanley D. *The Committee of One Million: "China Lobby" Politics, 1953–1971.* New York: Columbia University Press, 1976.

Bailey, Thomas A. *The Man in the Street: The Impact of American Public Opinion on Foreign Policy.* New York: Macmillan, 1948.

Baker, Roscoe. *The American Legion and American Foreign Policy.* New York: Bookman Associates, 1954.

Barnet, Richard J. *Roots of War: The Men and Institutions behind U.S. Foreign Policy.* New York: Atheneum, 1972.

Bauer, Raymond; Pool, Ithiel de Sola; and Dexter, Lewis A. *American Business and Public Policy: The Politics of Foreign Trade.* New York: Atherton Press, 1967.

Borg, Dorothy. *The United States and the Far Eastern Crisis of 1933–1938.* Cambridge: Harvard University Press, 1964.

Braestrup, Peter. *Big Story: How the American Press and Television Reported and Interpreted the Crisis of Tet 1968 in Vietnam and Washington.* Boulder: Westview Press, 1977.

Bruner, Jerome S. *Mandate from the People*. New York: Duell, Sloan, & Pearce, 1944.

Buchanan, William, and Cantril, Hadley. *How Nations See Each Other: A Study in Public Opinion*. Urbana: University of Illinois Press, 1953.

Cantril, Albert H., and Roll, Charles W., Jr. *Hopes and Fears of the American People*. New York: Universe Books, 1971.

Cantril, Hadley. *The Human Dimension*. New Brunswick: Rutgers University Press, 1967.

Cantril, Hadley, and Strunk, Mildred. *Public Opinion, 1935–1946*. Princeton: Princeton University Press, 1951.

Chadwin, Mark Lincoln. *The Hawks of World War II*. Chapel Hill: University of North Carolina Press, 1968.

Chatfield, Charles. *For Peace and Justice: Pacifism in America, 1914–1941*. Knoxville: University of Tennessee Press, 1971.

————, ed. *Peace Movements in America*. New York: Schocken Books, 1973.

Chester, Edward A. *Sectionalism, Politics, and American Diplomacy*. Metuchen, N.J.: Scarecrow Press, 1975.

Chittick, William O. *State Department, Press, and Pressure Groups*. New York: Wiley-Interscience, 1970.

Cohen, Bernard C. *The Press and Foreign Policy*. Princeton: Princeton University Press, 1963.

————. *The Public's Impact on Foreign Policy*. Boston: Little, Brown, 1973.

Cole, Wayne S. *America First: The Battle Against Intervention*. Madison: University of Wisconsin Press, 1953.

Cottrell, Leonard S., Jr., and Eberhart, Sylvia. *American Opinion on World Affairs in the Atomic Age*. Princeton: Princeton University Press, 1948.

Crabb, Cecil V., Jr. *Policy-Makers and Critics: Conflicting Theories of American Foreign Policy*. New York: Praeger, 1976.

Culbert, David H. *News for Everyman; Radio and Foreign Affairs in Thirties America.* Westport, Conn.: Greenwood Press, 1976.

Curti, Merle. *American Philanthropy Abroad: A History.* New Brunswick: Rutgers University Press, 1963.

Dawson, Raymond H. *The Decision to Aid Russia, 1941.* Chapel Hill: University of North Carolina Press, 1959.

DeConde, Alexander, ed. *Isolation and Security.* Durham: Duke University Press, 1957.

Diggins, John P. *Mussolini and Fascism: The View from America.* Princeton: Princeton University Press, 1972.

Divine, Robert A. *American Immigration Policy, 1924–1952.* New Haven: Yale University Press, 1957.

————. *The Illusion of Neutrality.* Chicago: University of Chicago Press, 1962.

————. *Second Chance: The Triumph of Internationalism in America during World War II.* New York: Atheneum, 1967.

————. *Foreign Policy and U.S. Presidential Elections, 1940–1948.* New York: New Viewpoints, 1974.

————. *Since 1945: Politics and Diplomacy in Recent American History.* New York: Wiley, 1975.

Filene, Peter G. *Americans and the Soviet Experiment, 1917–1933.* Cambridge: Harvard University Press, 1967.

Fleming, Denna F. *The United States and the World Court.* Garden City, N.Y.: Doubleday, 1955.

Flynn, George Q. *Roosevelt and Romanism: Catholics and American Diplomacy, 1937–1945.* Westport, Conn.: Greenwood Press, 1976.

Free, Lloyd A., and Cantril, Hadley. *The Political Beliefs of Americans: A Study of Public Opinion.* New Brunswick: Rutgers University Press, 1968.

Friedman, Donald J. *The Road from Isolation: The Campaign of the American Committee for Non-Participation in Japanese*

Aggression, 1938–1941. Cambridge: Harvard East Asian Monographs, 1968.

Gaddis, John Lewis. *The United States and the Origins of the Cold War, 1941–1947*. New York: Columbia University Press, 1972.

Gallup, George H. *The Gallup Poll, 1935–1971*. New York: Random House, 1972.

Gerson, Louis L. *The Hyphenate in Recent American Politics and Diplomacy*. Lawrence: University of Kansas Press, 1964.

Graber, Doris A. *Public Opinion, the President, and Foreign Policy*. New York: Holt, Rinehart & Winston, 1968.

Guttmann, Allen. *The Wound in the Heart: America and the Spanish Civil War*. New York: Free Press, 1962.

Harris, Louis. *The Anguish of Change*. New York: Norton, 1973.

Hero, Alfred O., Jr. *Americans in World Affairs*. Boston: World Peace Foundation, 1959.

———. *The Southerner and World Affairs*. Baton Rouge: Louisiana State University Press, 1965.

———. *American Religious Groups View Foreign Policy: Trends in Rank-and-File Opinion, 1937–1969*. Durham: Duke University Press, 1973.

Hero, Alfred O., Jr., and Starr, Emil. *The Reuther-Meany Foreign Policy Dispute: Union Leaders and Members View World Affairs*. Dobbs Ferry, N.Y.: Oceana, 1970.

Hess, Garry R. *America Encounters India, 1941–1947*. Baltimore: Johns Hopkins Press, 1971.

Hoag, C. Leonard. *Preface to Preparedness: The Washington Disarmament Conference and Public Opinion*. Washington, D.C.: Public Affairs Press, 1941.

Howe, Russell Warren, and Trott, Sarah Hays. *The Power Peddlers: How Lobbyists Mold America's Foreign Policy*. Garden City, N.Y.: Doubleday, 1977.

Iriye, Akira, ed. *Mutual Images: Essays in American-Japanese Relations*. Cambridge: Harvard University Press, 1975.

Isaacs, Harold R. *Scratches on Our Minds: American Images of China and India.* New York: John Day, 1958.

Johnson, Sheila K. *American Attitudes toward Japan, 1941–1975.* Washington, D.C.: AEI-Hoover, 1975.

Johnson, Walter. *The Battle against Isolation.* Chicago: University of Chicago Press, 1944.

Jonas, Manfred. *Isolationism in America, 1935–1941.* Ithaca: Cornell University Press, 1966.

Jones, Joseph M. *The Fifteen Weeks.* New York: Viking, 1955.

Kennan, George F. *American Diplomacy, 1900–1950.* Chicago: University of Chicago Press, 1951.

Key, V. O., Jr. *Public Opinion and American Democracy.* New York: Knopf, 1961.

Kimball, Warren F. *The Most Unsordid Act: Lend-Lease, 1939–1941.* Baltimore: Johns Hopkins Press, 1969.

Korvig, Bennett. *The Myth of Liberation: East-Central Europe in U.S. Diplomacy and Politics since 1941.* Baltimore: Johns Hopkins Press, 1973.

Kuehl, Warren F. *Seeking World Order: The United States and International Organization to 1920.* Nashville: Vanderbilt University Press, 1969.

Landecker, Manfred. *The President and Public Opinion: Leadership in Foreign Affairs.* Washington, D.C.: Public Affairs Press, 1968.

Larson, Cedric, and Mock, James R. *Words That Won the War: The Story of the Committee on Public Information, 1917–1919.* Princeton: Princeton University Press, 1939.

Lasch, Christopher. *The American Liberals and the Russian Revolution.* New York: Columbia University Press, 1962.

Leigh, Michael. *Mobilizing Consent: Public Opinion and American Foreign Policy, 1937–1947.* Westport, Conn.: Greenwood Press, 1976.

Levering, Ralph B. *American Opinion and the Russian Alliance,*

1939–1945. Chapel Hill: University of North Carolina Press, 1976.

Link, Arthur S. *Wilson the Diplomatist*. Baltimore: Johns Hopkins Press, 1957.

Lippmann, Walter. *Essays in the Public Philosophy*. Boston: Little, Brown, 1955.

Lydgate, William A. *What America Thinks*. New York: Crowell, 1944.

Markel, Lester, ed. *Public Opinion and Foreign Policy*. New York: Harper, 1949.

May, Ernest R. *"Lessons" of the Past: The Use and Misuse of History in American Foreign Policy*. New York: Oxford University Press, 1973.

Menefee, Selden. *Assignment: U.S.A.* New York: Reynal & Hitchcock, 1943.

Minott, Rodney G. *Peerless Patriots: Organized Veterans and the Spirit of Americanism*. Washington, D.C.: Public Affairs Press, 1962.

Morgenthau, Hans J. *In Defense of the National Interest*. New York: Knopf, 1951.

Mueller, John E. *War, Presidents and Public Opinion*. New York: Wiley, 1973.

Neumann, William L. *America Encounters Japan: From Perry to MacArthur*. Baltimore: Johns Hopkins Press, 1963.

Offner, Arnold A. *American Appeasement: United States Foreign Policy and Germany, 1933–1938*. Cambridge: Harvard University Press, 1969.

Osgood, Robert Endicott. *Ideals and Self-Interest in America's Foreign Relations*. Chicago: University of Chicago Press, 1953.

Parenti, Michael. *The Anti-Communist Impulse*. New York: Random House, 1969.

Peterson, H. C., and Fite, Gilbert C. *Opponents of War, 1917–1918*. Madison: University of Wisconsin Press, 1957.

Radosh, Ronald. *American Labor and United States Foreign Policy*. New York: Random House, 1969.

Roper, Elmo. *You and Your Leaders: Their Actions and Your Reactions, 1936–1956*. New York: William Morrow, 1957.

Rosenau, James N. *Public Opinion and Foreign Policy*. New York: Random House, 1961.

————, ed. *Domestic Sources of Foreign Policy*. New York: Free Press, 1967.

Scott, William A., and Withey, Stephen B. *The United States and the United Nations: The Public View, 1945–1955*. New York: Carnegie Endowment for International Peace, 1958.

Small, Melvin, ed. *Public Opinion and Historians: Interdisciplinary Perspectives*. Detroit: Wayne State University Press, 1970.

Smith, Charles W., Jr. *Public Opinion in a Democracy*. New York: Prentice-Hall, 1939.

Smith, M. Brewster; Bruner, Jerome S.; and White, Robert W. *Opinions and Personality*. New York: Wiley, 1956.

Snetsinger, John. *Truman, the Jewish Vote, and the Creation of Israel*. Stanford, Calif.: Hoover Institution Press, 1974.

Steele, A. J. *The American People and China*. New York: McGraw-Hill, 1966.

Tupper, Eleanor, and McReynolds, George E. *Japan in American Opinion*. New York: Macmillan, 1937.

Waltz, Kenneth. *Foreign Policy and Democratic Politics*. Boston: Little, Brown, 1967.

Watts, William, and Free, Lloyd A., eds. *State of the Nation*. New York: Universe Books, 1973.

Weisbord, Robert G. *Ebony Kinship: Africa, Africans, and the Afro-American*. Westport, Conn.: Greenwood Press, 1973.

Weissberg, Robert. *Public Opinion and Popular Government*. Englewood Cliffs, N.J.: Prentice-Hall, 1976.

Wilson, Joan Hoff. *American Business and Foreign Policy, 1920–1933*. Lexington: University Press of Kentucky, 1971.

Wiltz, John E. *In Search of Peace: The Senate Munitions Inquiry, 1934–36.* Baton Rouge: Louisiana State University Press, 1963.

Wittner, Lawrence S. *The American Peace Movement, 1941–1960.* New York: Columbia University Press, 1969.

INDEX

Acheson, Dean, 25
activists, 21, 87, 146, 154
  anti-Vietnam, 133-136
  in Cold War period, 105-106, 109-110
Addams, Jane, 60
AFL-CIO, 33, 123, 142
Agar, Herbert, 67
age, policy positions and, 127, 139
Agnew, Spiro, 136
alliances
  reversals of, after 1945, 105
  Western, after World War II, 121, 124, 145
Allison, Graham T., 139
Almond, Gabriel A., 149, 163
Alsop, Joseph, 114
America First, 71
American Association for the United Nations, 110
American Council on Judaism, 71, 100
American Federation of Labor, 54, 62
American Friends Legislative Service, 50
American Friends of Italy, 63
American Friends Service Committee, 106
American-Israel Public Affairs Committee, 142
American-Italian Union, 63
American Jewish Committee, 61
American Jewish Conference, 100
American Jewish Congress, 61, 62
American Legion, 33, 40, 54, 123, 133
American Zionist Emergency Council, 100

Americans for Democratic Action, 126
anti-Semitism, in Nazi Germany, 61-62, 68
anxiety period (1946–1962), 92-93, 112
Arafat, Yasir, 142
Armstrong, Hamilton Fish, 37, 58
Ashbrook, John, 132
assumptions, dominant
  changes in, 31, 66, 120-122, 131-133, 136-137, 139, 155-163
  policy options and, 30, 104, 124-125, 131, 149
  role of public opinion and, 152
Atlantic Charter, 90
atomic weapons and energy, 92, 93, 95-96, 106, 110-111, 112
attentive public, 20-21, 23, 24-25, 29, 39, 42, 43, 47, 53, 66, 84, 95, 99-100, 114, 122, 125, 141, 152, 154, 157, 162-163
  see also activists; organizations

Bay of Pigs, 117
Beard, Charles, 65-66
Becker, Carl L., 50
Berrigan, Philip and Daniel, 136
bipartisanship, 66, 79, 80, 101, 102
black Americans, 63-64, 131
Black Muslims, 27
Blum, John Morton, 89
B'nai B'rith, 61
Bolshevism, 41-42
boycotts, 60, 62, 63, 74
Bread for the World, 146
Brezinski, Zbigniew, 146
Brown, Lester R., 146
Buck, Pearl, 59